INVL
On the Internet

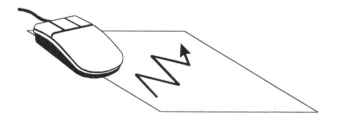

Scott Weren

NET.WORKS

NET.WORKS

Net.Works
P.O.Box 200, Harrogate
HG1 2YR England
Fax: 01423-526035
Email: sales@net-works.co.uk
http://www.net-works.co.uk/books.htm

ISBN 1-873668-66-X

Contents

Preface

The sheer popularity of the Internet, and the almost exponential increase in its usership, ironically poses its greatest threat. Apart from periodically grinding to a halt, it is becoming increasingly difficult to locate anything of use.

Even a carefully constructed Boolean search will render many pages of results, and most of those will be complete rubbish. Indeed, on several occasions I've looked for a site that I know exists, but found myself incapable of locating it because of similarly named sites whose owners have spent time getting them to the top of the search engine's lists.

It was with this problem in view that the ***...on the Internet*** series was conceived. In each book you will find a completely impartial review of the websites in each category. The aim is to save the user time, money and a large amount of frustration. If you can flick through this book and then quickly access a site that you need, then it has done its job.

Happy (rapid) surfing!

Scott

Also in the same series:
> *Sex on the Internet*
> *Golf on the Internet*
> *Football on the Internet*
> *Gambling on the Internet*

Click Here

The Internet, and in particular the World Wide Web, seem to be expanding at an exponential rate. The amount of information that is available to anyone who logs-on is absolutely astounding. A good deal of that information is particularly useful for investors of all sorts - experienced, inexperienced, professional and amateur.

It is the sheer volume of information available on the Internet which is proving to be a hindrance to its effective use. You can no longer rely on a quick visit to a search engine as a way of finding the site that you are looking for. Even if you enter specific keywords and construct an ideal Boolean search at your favourite search site, the web pages that you are hoping to find may be buried on the fourteenth of fifteenth page of search results. And how many times have you looked that far into searches that you've generated?

With the help of this publication you will now be able to quickly lay your hands on information directly relevant to investing. It should cut down your on-line time immensely and certainly reduce the stress of not being able to find something that you know is there. The Internet offers many advantages to the private investor and most of these are centred around the quick access to volumes of information. So using this publication effectively could give you that crucial time advantage over your fellow investors.

Using the site and information contained in Investing on the Internet you will be able to develop a personalised investment strategy that will stand you in good stead during this period of rapid technological advancement. There are plenty of books on the shelves which deal with investment strategies and how to go about generating large amounts of money. And there are also a range of titles which deal with using the Internet. But Investing on the Internet pulls the two together in a sensible manner and reviews sites that could be of interest.

You may be heartened to know that neither the author of this book nor the company that publishes it have any interest in financial services. The book is not being written to promote an author's investment system or a company's product, services or web site. It is totally independent and the opinions given are purely those of the author who has been investing with the aid of the information from the Internet, both directly and indirectly, for the last six years. In terms of the Internet, and its rapid development, that makes them wizened old veterans!

This publication is designed to give you all the instructions and information that you will ever need in order to go about investing on the Internet. You could read it from the front cover to the back and gain an overall view before you even go on-line. But you will equally find it just as easy to read bits at a time, dropping in and out as and when you have time.

As I said earlier, the main advantage that the web offers Internet investors over those who never go on-line is the quantity and quality of information that can be gathered and read in a timely manner. This facility, based on computers around the world, almost puts you on a level footing with the professional city players who are frequently shown on news items staring at banks of screens. Via the Internet you can actually access the same information that these traders will be looking at and have the same news bulletins fed to your screen so you can act at the same time or even before the big time investors have had a chance to move the prevailing prices.

Say, for example, you get up at 6.30 am. You make your breakfast and grab a cup of coffee as you log onto your Internet account. In your in-tray you have copies of your personalised morning newspapers and investment magazines. As you glance through them you notice that a particular information technology company has reported disappointing sales in the last quarter. You have been watching this sector for the last few years and seen the prices soar to levels that you believe are too high.

You now fire up your browser and visit a site which gives you a free chart with the company's stock prices movements over the last three years. Sure enough it has shown a rapid increase in value. Next you log onto a site that is showing real time stock market data and you see that the company's share price has dropped by nearly 20% on the breaking news. It is now within a price range that you consider to be an opportunity.

Next job is to go along and get a copy of the company's report. You do this from two sources: the company's official web site and a third party site which offers commentary on recently published annual reports. Armed with the background data you can now check into any number of sites which will offer an opinion on the stock's movement. After viewing these comments you decide that things aren't as bad as they appear and it could well be worth jumping into the stock.

Before you commit your money, however, you visit a site which offers free technical analysis software and run a couple of routines. Sure enough the buying signals are clearly indicated.

Then, as you are finishing your analysis, your computer beeps as a push technology site which you have subscribed to sends another bulletin on the same company. They have just announced a major new contract that will see them expanding for the next decade. You have received this information at the same time as all the major financial institutions.

So without hesitating you log onto your on-line broker's site and immediately place an order for the purchase of shares in the information technology company you have been researching. The city boys are still on the phone trying to move large blocks of stock and prices have barely had a chance to react to the latest news bulletin. You have beaten the market and can log off in the knowledge that the price will be increasing before you even have a chance to get into your car and go to work.

This may only be a fictional example but it is one that is achievable by any investor within Internet access.

All of this sounds almost too good to be true, but it isn't. Looking through the following pages you realise that you too can use the Internet to improve your investing performance.

However, from time to time, you will come across particular offerings which also look too good to be true. In this instance, they probably are. Investing on the Internet is speeded up by the fact that you are not dealing with human beings and all their facilities. Technology is being used as it should be to cut out all the rubbish and get straight to the salient point. But beware, this faceless interaction also provides opportunities for fraudsters.

In various dark corners of the Internet you will find dangerous and costly traps aimed at liberating you from your savings. There aren't any more or any less of these schemes on the Internet than there are in "real life", but they are there nonetheless and you should beware of anything that looks like a get rich quick scheme.

Investment on the Internet helps you:

✔ Subscribe to newsgroups and mailing lists that are relevant to your investment strategies.

✔ Use push technology to receive new detailed and specific info direct to your desktop.

✔ Subscribe to investment related sites which will give you market commentary along with advice tips and offers.

✔ Monitor real time or delayed prices for almost any financial instrument.

✔ Study past performance data and charts and carry out technical and fundamental analysis.

✔ Research industry specific information gaining valuable detailed background information.

✔ View company annual reports and broker recommendations.

✔ Manage your own portfolio and automatically up date the prices contained in it.

✔ Buy and sell almost any financial instrument that exists at the lowest commission fees you will find anywhere in the world.

Investment Fundamentals

MoneyWeb

www.moneyweb.co.uk

> Overall rating - ***
> Speed - Medium
> Advertising Level - High
> Free

On the surface this looks like a rather amateur affair with bright cartoony images. It is also not very well structured as you need to scroll down the first page for three or four screens before you reach the bottom. This is a shame because quite a lot of the information that is there is fairly useful.

There are lots of good basics on all matters concerning pensions, mortgages, investments, life insurance, etc. The site contains features and essays with topical articles written from people within the financial services industry. It is aimed at the UK private investor with quite a lot of information directed at "industry professionals". There are a series of calculators on the site including currency converters, single monthly premium calculators for pensions and benefits scheme calculators.

If you look around you will find some investment humour, some details and links on tax and an investment quiz.

Invest-o-rama!

www.investorama.com

Overall rating - ****
Speed - Fast
Advertising Level - Low
Free

Essentially this site is a collection of links to on line sources with investment information. It touts itself as a directory and at the time of writing included around 10,000 links in more than 120 categories. The site includes a good investors glossary of more than 500 words, phrases and abbreviations and personal finance software that you are able to download for free. There is an interactive tool that will help you plan for your financial freedom in the future as well as standard investment news.

Some of the more advanced tools that you will find on this site include a free portfolio tracker and free advance charting with customisable parameters. If you are looking to research a particular stock you will find plenty of links to research sites and around 5,000 links to the web sites of publicly quoted companies. Absolutely necessary for a site this size is a good search facility and this is provided along with the ability to search other sites from the home page. Finally if you want even more investment information you are able to subscribe to a free e-mail newsletter.

Money World

www.moneyworld.co.uk

Overall rating - ***
Speed - Medium
Advertising Level - Medium
Free

If you are looking to buy and sell shares on the Internet or just keep an eye on your hot-stocks you will find the basics on this site.

The is a host of valuable books helping you manage money better including a personal tax calculator and another directory of finance web sites. There is news from around the world which you may find more useful than information on the best mortgage deals which looks like a sales hunt than anything.

If you want to joint the Money World Club you can do from the site and it is free. Not many of the benefits are Internet related however and you will simply benefit from discounts on products that you probably would not want to buy normally.

You should not let this trivia divert you however from a decent site which gives many of the facilities a beginner will be looking for.

Investor Guide

investorguide
the leading guide to investing on the web

www.investorguide.com

Overall rating - ****
Speed - Fast
Advertising Level - Low
Free

A regularly up dated site that is one of the leaders in the field on the web. The news is updated every day as are the commons in the research area. You can access real time quotes and historical charts for a large range of companies and indices. It is slightly US-centric but of general use to everyone around the world. To get to know the site quickly take the three minute tour which will show you some of the salient points.

When you have finished the tour make sure that you return to have a look at the question and answer centre. There is over 1,000 investing questions that have been answered in this area and it is well worth having a look and make sure that you print it off or view it off line. Also in the learning arena you will find discussion groups and investment club details plus 10 principles of investing, overall strategy tips, advice on taking advice, calculators and a portfolio tracker which are all serviced through links. If you would like to get more you can also register for the free on line investor guide e-mail newsletter.

Investor Web

www.financialweb.co/investorweb.asp

> Overall rating - ***
> Speed - Slow
> Advertising Level - Medium
> Free

InvestorWeb is part of the wider financial web site which is fairly clean cut in design but also rather dower. Since the site gets straight to the point so will this review and you will find quotes, charts, information on bonds and the market, an editorial section, stock-pics, details on mutual funds, earnings, research, an investors book store and some humour.

Business Headlines

It is absolutely vital that you stay in touch with the business news if you want to make sure you are maximising your investment returns. These days, if you miss a news blip, you can very quickly find yourself nursing a big loss.

The Internet can solve your problems. It is now easier than ever to receive the same information direct to your desktop, as the professional traders are receiving.

Bloomberg

ww.bloomberg.com

> Overall rating - *****
> Speed - Fast
> Advertising Level - Low
> Free

A hot bed of business news based in the US (regional sites are linked). From the opening

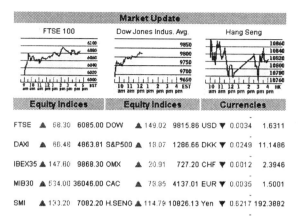

FTSE	▲ 68.30	6085.00	DOW	▲ 149.02	9815.86	USD	▼ 0.0034	1.6311
DAXI	▲ 66.48	4863.81	S&P500	▲ 18.07	1286.66	DKK	▼ 0.0249	11.1486
IBEX35	▲ 147.60	9868.30	OMX	▲ 20.91	727.20	CHF	▼ 0.0012	2.3946
MIB30	▲ 534.00	36046.00	CAC	▲ 78.85	4137.01	EUR	▼ 0.0035	1.5001
SMI	▲ 133.20	7082.20	H.SENG	▲ 114.79	10826.13	Yen	▼ 0.6217	192.3882

page you can access the latest, and we mean latest, business stories. There is also a useful news byte section relating to the current 'Hot Stocks', saving you searching through the rest of the news, plus the main worldwide indices (Dow, S&P500, Nasdaq, FTSE, Nikkei) and an hourly chart of the Dow Jones Industrial Average.

One page down you'll be able to locate lots more including market information on bonds, further indices, market sectors, futures and currencies. Connect to any of the other Bloomberg sites in the UK, Italy, Japan, Latin America, Australia and Germany, and subscribe to Bloomberg *Personal Finance* magazine.

Business Wire

www.businesswire.com

Current busines headlines as they occur. The home page lists headlines from the business world and links to the story provider. This is a useful way of scanning all news that's coming in and then progressing to the full story if you want more details. You can display headlines by date and by period, say the last five hours. You can also filter the headlines down by region, but this sometimes loses relevant stories with much wider bearing in the world.

| Overall rating - ***** |
| Speed - Fast |
| Advertising - Medium |
| Free |

By glancing down a panel, you can navigate your way through the site to obtain headlines relating to specific industries such as high-tech, health, banking, energy and automotive. Alternatively you may go for corporate specific news and back-up information such as corporate profiles. Separate sections deal with news releases, business photos and executive viewpoints.

CNN

www.cnnfn.com

> Overall rating - ***
> Speed - Medium
> Advertising Level - Medium
> Free

The financial news offering from the giant media network. Here you can locate hot stories, market information and index movements. The headlines tend to be generalised as they are re-written, but the scope is fairly impressive. One of the best areas to view is the news from small businesses, as this is often hard to come by as an ordinary investor.

World business gives a more global viewpoint than the obvious US bias apparent on the site - surprising for such an international company. 'Industry Watch' is another handy way of grouping the details you may want to avoid information overload.

NewsEdge

www.newspage.com

> Overall rating - ***
> Speed - Fast
> Advertising Level - Low
> Free and pay

News headlines are free but you may need to pay for the full story depending on how it is rated. The main story is followed by links to around five other main business related stories of the day. Also on the home page, you'll find the state of the FTSE, NASDAQ, NYSE and S&P500.

Further into the site, you'll find news from specific industries: business and finance, computing, energy, healthcare, internet, mass media, networking, telecomms, industrials and general. A search engine is provided to look up company details by name or ticker. More general news is available, such as sports, politics and world news to lighten the info load, and a few investment tips are occasionally thrown in for good value.

THE WALL STREET JOURNAL INTERACTIVE EDITION.

The Wall Street Journal

www.wsj.com

Overall rating - *****
Speed - Fast
Advertising Level - Medium
Pay with extensive free areas

This is the interactive edition of the old faithful. Read all the latest news discover how the market is performing and take a look at some of the main stories in the days printed version of the Wall Street Journal. There is a list of all the reports contained within the Journal plus four or five that you can access for free.

If you wish to subscribe then you can receive personalised news, a stock portfolio monitor, 20 minutes delayed stock quotes, daily market reports, company profiles, backgrounds, financial overviews and economic indicators. You also have the ability to search the last two weeks issues of the Journal.

FINANCIAL TIMES

Where information becomes intelligence

Financial Times

www.ft.com

Overall rating - ***
Speed - Slow
Advertising Level - Medium
Free

A free site once you have subscribed - which is why this site losses a star it would otherwise have (we've all got more than enough usernames and passwords to handle, thankyou). Euro-centric news makes a refreshing change for those investing in the UK and mainland Europe. At a glance you can find breaking news, latest euro prices, special reports from around the world and market data (prices and indices). On top of the news, personal finance articles are updated regularly, business celebrities are interviewed and many parts of the site have been archived.

As you would expect of the FT, it's strength lies in it's coverage of the markets. Nowhere else will you find all of these in one place: Capital markets, currencies, commodities, emerging markets, equities, managed funds, currencies, offshore funds, indices and futures?

New York Times

www.nytimes.com

Overall rating - ***
Speed - Fast
Advertising Level - Medium
Free

A very extensive site bringing you virtually everything from the printed version of the New York Times. The times on the Web, apart from being a good read, brings you the days top business stories indications of how the markets are performing and international business news. All the stories are indexed in categories and there is a key word search facility. A very good site of use to any investor with US stocks in their portfolio.

The New York Times
ON THE WEB

Daily Telegraph

www.telegraph.co.uk

UK business news brought to the Net by one of the UK's broadsheets. Find city headlines, market reports,

> Overall rating - **
> Speed - Fast
> Advertising - Medium
> Free

share prices (delayed) a financial directory, a business directory, the City diary and, of course, the cartoon Alex. Business headlines appear with an exec summary and a link to the fuller story.

Investors Chronicle

www.investorschronicle.co.uk

> Overall rating - *
> Speed - Fast
> Advertising Level - Medium
> Pay

A hefty subscription will get you the on-line version of this respected UK investment publication. Lots of business news accompanied by investment advice. However, most of the information can be found for free on other sites. The proliferation of terms and conditions plus disclaimers sets the scene all too well.

On the plus side, the depth of back-issue archives saves the day, allowing you to perform keyword and company searches. If you are doing serious research on a specific company and how it has featured in the news then this site is a valid alternative to spending hours online.

WebFinance

www.webfiance.com

Overall rating - **
Speed - Fast
Advertising Level - Low
Pay with free headlines

A daily Web site produce in conjunction with the Buy weekly print publication. On the front page you will get some free daily news service headlines but you will need to be subscriber to get the full details behind the story. On top of the news items you will find an extensive series of features which is enhanced by the ability to search the archives. Although a lot of news is presented on the site there isn't too much comment and you are left to work out what it all means for yourself if you can decipher the spin.

The Economist

www.economist.com

Overall rating - **
Speed - Slow
Advertising Level - Medium
Pay

Basically gives you a list of articles that are available in the printed version. Selected items are available on-line with one or two surveys. You can also access the leader articles and a business summary.

The useful section tells you what is new on the site and you are able to search archives of articles back to 1995. You will also occasionally find a new subject which is treated in more depth with an economist briefing.

Do It Yourself

With several hundred million web pages already in existence the Internet is rapidly becoming the working definition of "information overload".

Investing on the Internet is clearly designed to take some of the burden of finding investment related sites off your shoulders. However smart investors will also want to develop their own information systems to use in parallel with information you will find in this publication.

Ideally this information system will have the capability of giving you the indicators that you will need to predict possible price movements and investment opportunities.

Your systems, of course, need to be designed so that the information you access regularly will be useful in both bull and bear markets, so no situation can arise where you were left wondering what to do. With your computer doing the bulk of the work this is perfectly possible with only a little bit of considered forethought.

An example of this might be the movement of bond yields and interest rates. Everyone knows that as interest rates drop investors pile their cash into the stock market. This cause prices to rise, by supply and demand, and provides ample opportunity for early investors to make good profits. Some also know that when bond yields decline a similar effect often takes place. But you would not normally dream of keeping track of bond yields because of the sheer drudgery of find bond prices in the newspaper and performing often complex calculations to discover whether an individual yield has gone down or up.

However by developing your own Internet information system you can either circumvent the whole process by looking for news of how bond yields are moving or use a spreadsheet and free on-line prices to make your own instant calculations.

But how do you go about setting up your own system and finding information such as current bond yields? The first step in finding your own investment sites has to be the commercial search engine. These sites are essentially a collection of web site addresses and indexation of individual web pages. Some review the sites which they provide on their pages and create extensive directories and catalogues. But most simply collect the information and offer it in an unfiltered and unedited manner through the use of "bots".

Modern search engines fall into three basic categories:

Passive search engines

These are probably more accurately referred to as directories. They rely on Internet users to give them details of sites they have created or found on the World Wide Web in order to build up a database. When they receive the submissions from individual surfers the search engine company visits the site that has been recommended and puts it into the correct section of their database with or without a review.

To find the details of the site in such a directory you need to find a main category and click you way through several layers of sub-categories before you come to the basic level of site.

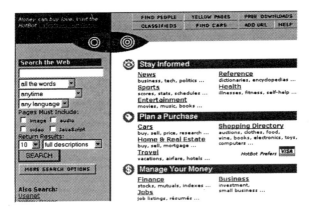

Active search engines

These engines rely on programmes known as "spiders" or "web robots" to index and categorise pages and sites. The bots travel out into the World Wide Web in search of new sites either on their own or with the prompting of web site creators. When it finds a site it downloads the information contained on the page and then automatically categorises the site according to what it has found. The way in which the site is categorised varies according to the particular search engine. The words and phrases which are extracted are then added to the database that is searched when you go to the engine.

METASEARCH

Put commas between word groups to treat them as phrases.

| Search | online banks | 50 | hits |

Find matches containing ○ This **phrase** ● **All** of these words ○ **Any** of these words

Match ● Only as complete words ○ Within other words also

Output: ● Verbose ○ Standard ○ Terse

Meta-search engine

This is a search engine that has a capability of searching several other search sites at the same time. By entering a single search term the meta-search then queries other search engines on the web to find out what they know about the term. The results are then collated and then de-duplicated before being presented on your screen. By creating sensible search strings you can save a lot of time by using these sites. Three meta-search engines that you might like to try include MetaCrawler which can be found at *www.metacrawler.com*, Meta-search which can be found at *www.metasearch.com* and, the rather oddly named, DogPile which is located at *www.dogpile.com*!

Better Searches

Over time you will find which search engine better suits your needs. Some produce more results than others, largely dependant on the size of their acquired database. One thing that they all have in common, though, is the fact that they will produce more pages as a result of your query than you will be able to look at. The initial result is that you are still faced with information overload. To help get over this you can use one or more of the following techniques:

- Search for a phrase or several words rather than just one word. For example, simply entering the word "money" and hitting the search button will produce several tens of millions of possible pages. But entering a phrase such as "money market deposit rates" will result in a much smaller list of possibilities.

- If a search engine allows, limit your search to one of the relevant directories. For example Excite has a category called "money and investing". This will prevent irrelevant hits sneaking in from other categories.

- Try a different way of writing what you are looking for (synonyms). For example, instead of searching for 'European commodity markets' you could try a search for 'European futures exchanges'.

- ● Use Boolean Operators to refine your initial searches.

Boolean Operators may sound complex but it isn't at all difficult to use them in your favour. Boolean logic has three fundamental concepts - AND, NOT, and OR.

AND will usually expand your search. It is used to link words so that the results you receive will contain both words. For example; news AND results will only return web pages that are stored in the database with both news and results as keywords.

NOT will generally limit your search. By linking words with the NOT Operator you will be able to exclude sites containing the second keyword. For example; news NOT results will return pages which include the keyword "news" so long as the word "results" is not used as well.

OR links words so that the search results contains either or both of the words. For example; news OR results will return pages that are filed under news, that are filed under results, and are filed under news and results.

Personalisation is the new key word

The "in thing" as far as search engines go is personalisation. Many of the major engines such as Yahoo (my.yahoo.com) and excite (my.excite.com) now allow you to customise what you see when you enter their site.

For the sake of about one hour's fiddling around you are able to set the search engine so that you receive news that is of interest to you. On top of that you are able to view stock prices that you specify by "ticker" and even keep track of your own portfolio.

Shares

I t's difficult to separate out specific sites relating just to stocks since virtually all investment sites include basic equities to some extent or other. Perhaps they could be defined as the sites left over when you subtract those relating to other investment vehicles such as bonds, futures, options and commodities?

One thing's for sure, information relating to stocks on the Internet is not difficult to come by. Some, however, are better than others - and you should find these following sites good launch-pad for your explorations.

Briefing.com

www.briefing.com

A marvelous site to all investors in the US markets. It gives quick concise objective analysis of important events affecting stocks and bonds updated throughout the day. Analysis of

Overall rating - *****
Speed - Fast
Advertising - Low
Pay with free area

individual stocks and the factors that it will affect the values in the future are given from a panel of experts. Whether you have just started investing on-line or a seasoned professional you will find that Briefing.com keeps you informed focused and ahead of the markets.

The free services include market comments with an incisive edge along with quotes and charts. You can manage your portfolio, look at sector ratings and view an economic calendar.

If you are willing to pay for the basic stock analysis service you will receive a constantly updated analysis of the US stock market throughout the day with information on upgrades and downgrades of stocks, stock splits, technical stock coverage, earnings news and analysis. It is a fast focused and insightful service.

The top of the range at Briefing.com is a professional service which provides in-depth fixed income and FX market coverage, live bond market commentary, rapid analysis of economic releases and much more. If you want to keep your finger on the pulse of the US market this is the place to be.

Electronic Share Information

www.esi.co.uk

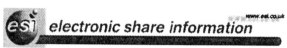

Everything you need to make your investment decisions on the UK market in one convenient place. Sights like this really do make it easy to track the markets, analyse stocks and manage your portfolio. The service is free with various levels of increased information if you are willing to pay. The free service offers stock prices updated eight times a day and a comprehensive price listing is posted after midnight.

The basic subscription package allows you to personalise a portfolio for tracking up to 100 shares and you receive a portfolio evaluation e-mailed to you in the morning. You receive accessed charts for nearly 5,000 different shares and daily unit trust prices.

The top package offers unlimited real time prices and a real-time multi-port-folio valuation services.

> Overall rating - *****
> Speed - Medium
> Advertising - Low
> Pay with free area

Asian Stocks Market Information

www.ppn.com.hk/asminfo.html

Overall rating - ***
Speed - Fast
Advertising Level - High
Free

The Pacific professional network brings you on line financial news, commercial intelligence and business opportunities from Australia, Hong Kong, India, Japan, Karachi, Korea, Malaysia, New Zealand, Singapore, Sri Lanka and Taiwan. Finding quality information on these emerging markets is often quite difficult but this site will give you the low down on the latest market moves.

Stock Club

stockclub.com

A set of interactive discussion forums on individual stocks in other investment topics. You will find diverse opinions and information a friendly uncluttered atmosphere com-

bined with a powerful search capability and e-mail service that will notify you immediately when a stock you are following is being discussed.

This is an excellent site which appears to be without any hidden agendas such as "Pick of the Week", "Investment Advice", "Associated Pay-for Newsletters", and advertising. It is so clean that you won't even find any cascading dialogue boxes or Javascript tricks opening up other windows. All discussions which take place on-line are kept for a minimum of one year.

Overall rating - *****
Speed - Fast
Advertising Level - None
Free

WallStreetView

www.wallstreetview.com

Overall rating - ***
Speed - Medium
Advertising Level - High
Free

This site describes itself as a financial portable site and has a very busy feel to it. From the front page you can access around 40 sites, with a selection of sites under the heading commentary, US stock exchanges, indices, research ideas, investment education, and company research. There are five search engines incorporated in the home site which allow you to track down details of company reports and to get online quotes.

There is also no shortage of links to financial news sites, those which offer stock ideas, financial briefing sites, and trading companies.

WallStreetView.com

NEW! MyPortfolio - Newswire - Book Store - Newsletters - Contest - Chat

Briefing	MorningCall	SignalWatch	StoryStocks	MarketWrap
StockIdeas	Preview	MarketCall	TradingIdeas	Bull-Market
TradingPit	MrktWatch	MostActive	Winners	Options
Research	Economic	Earnings	SECFilings	IPO's

$tockPlayer

www.stockplayer.com

> Overall rating - ****
> Speed - Medium
> Advertising Level - Medium
> Free pay for newsletter

A business and financial Web site that brings detailed information about stocks on Wall Street. Stockplayer.com profiles various companies that the owners feel have tremendous growth potential.

Whilst you are free to take notice of their stock picks you will probably find the other pieces of information on this site of more use: a market snap shot of the movement of the Dow Jones, S&P 500, and Nasdaq markets, breaking news, beginners advice, a glossary of terms, and information on Internet trading for beginners.

If you do find their tips useful you can view quotes and charts relating to the company and subscribe to the Stock Player newsletter.

Savvy Chat

nternet newsgroups are meeting places where like minded people gather together to discuss relevant issues.

There are currently more than 20,000 accessible newsgroups to discuss subjects ranging from international importance to the totally trivial. Around 1,000 of these newsgroups are of interest to the Internet investor.

Each of these groups will be accessed regularly by like-minded people from around the world. They provide a perfect place for you to find out what other Internet investors think about a particular subject.

For example, two major banks may announce a merger. Is this a good thing or a bad thing and will the shares rise in value or drop like a stone? Why not pop along to a relevant newsgroup to see what everybody else is saying.

At first you may be a bit reticent to let other people know your views but you can be sure that others will not share the same level of shyness. So expect to see a frank exchange of views from a range of people with different ideologies and investing beliefs. And since stock market movements depend upon such views, what better place to form your own opinions?

Tracing a relevant newsgroup is fairly simple. The first part of the group's name will tell you whether it has been set up to discuss alternative subjects (*alt*), miscellaneous topics (*misc*), and business subjects (*biz*). The next portion of the name will tell you the main subject that is being discussed within the newsgroup. For example *mis.invest* will be a miscellaneous newsgroup set up to discuss general investment.

Any further additions to the name of the newsgroup will indicate some form of speciality. For example *misc.invest.futures* is a sub-section of those belonging to the miscellaneous investment newsgroup who wish to discuss the particular subject of futures.

Hanging around the newsgroups, known as "lurking", is also an ideal way of finding out about other web sites. During the discussions you will see other users mention web sites that they have been to and visited or even some that they have created themselves.

If you see any that catch your eye why not visit them and add them to your "favourites" list if you find them useful.

A word of warning, at this point, would be useful for anyone who is not familiar with newsgroups. It is considered extremely bad manners to barge into a newsgroup and simply ask a question or demand some information. If you do this without observing the general level of discussion you are likely to be "flamed" and find your in-tray filling up with angry messages from the more experienced newsgroup users.

Most newsgroups establish an FAQ file of frequently asked questions to avoid such occurrences. Take a look at the group's FAQ file and see if anybody has already answered your query.

General Investing

acc.sbell.usa-today.invest
Forum originating with newspaper USA Today, discussion on investing.

alt.investResources,
information, and opportunities for investors and market watchers.

alt.invest.market.crash

Research and information services for investors, along with discussion on market strategies.

alt.invest.technical-analysis.omega

Technical market analysis and other resources for investors

misc.invest.financial-plan

Discussion, advice, and resources about market strategies.

misc.invest.miscInvestment

advice, services, market opportunities.

misc.invest.technical

Investment advice for individual investors and market professionals.

usa-today.invest

For businesses seeking investors.

Futures & Options

gov.us.topic.finance.securities

Rules, regulations, procedures governing securities.

misc.invest.futures
Advice and services on futures trading.

misc.invest.options
Advice and discussion on analysing and trading options.

Stocks

alt.invest.penny-stock
Services, advice for individual investors

alt.invest.penny-stocks
Investment discussion, services and advice for small investors.

misc.invest.stocks
Investment advice, resources, and discussion about the stock market

Mutual Funds

misc.invest.mutual-funds
Mutual fund advice and services.

Taxes

misc.taxes.moderated

Derivatives

Often thought of as the playground for rocket scientists, the derivatives markets have seen a huge explosion in growth. One day it may all end in tears, as most of today's financial scandals seem to centre around derivatives and their mis-use.

If you fancy yourself as a rouge trader take a look around the web to see how to gear your profits and losses beyond everyone's comprehension...

NumaWeb

www.numa.com

```
Overall rating - *****
Speed - Fast
Advertising Level - Low
Free
```

Describes itself as the Internet's home page for financial derivatives and there is no arguing there. Whether your are a derivatives beginner or a practising expert you will find something of use on this site. For the beginner there is details of courses and conferences but there is also an on-line tutorial which will tell you the basics of derivative and if you are unsure of what everyone is talking about you will find a dictionary of acronyms used in the derivatives world. In the main index you will also find details on the futures and options exchanges and guides as to option strategies you can adopt.

Once you have picked up the derivatives baton you might want to make use of the calculator for options prices warrants and convertible bonds and then pop along to the excellent numa derivatives forum which is populated by numerous experts on the subject.

If you have not had your fill of derivatives by then pop along to the derivatives book shop and subscribe to the derivatives announcement service which will come direct to your desktop. And finally if you want to loose somebody else's money rather than your own you take a look at the employment index.

Contingency Analysis

www.contingencyanalysis.com

Overall rating - ***
Speed - Medium
Advertising Level - Low
Free

Over 1,000 pages of information on financial risk management. Topics on this site include value at risk, derivative instruments, credit risk and financial engineering.

It is put together by Glyn Holton who is a consultant in the financial risk management arena. On his site you will find the fundamentals of risk management with many on-line research papers looking at particular issues.

Although the site positions itself as a forum where professionals can discuss financial risk management over the Internet there is something here for beginners and it will give you a good overview of the subject if you do not know your Delta from your Gamma and your VAR.

Applied Derivative Trading

www.adtrading.com

Overall rating - ****
Speed - Fast
Advertising Level - Medium
Free

This is a free monthly magazine all about the aspects of trading and using derivatives around the world. It is only published on the Internet but is read by more than 12,000 readers over 119 different countries.

All the vital topics such as dealing and trading techniques, exchange traded derivatives news, fundamental analysis, the psychology of trading and the development of the OTC derivatives markets are covered in addition to articles on each specific derivative.

The Derivatives 'zine

www.margrabe.com

Overall rating - ***
Speed - Fast
Advertising Level - Low
Free

A much less polished site than the applied derivatives trading effort but still worth a look. Tot start with take a look at the derivatives dictionary which will help you understand everything else from then on.

Unique to this site is the extensive number of links to derivatives sites on the World Wide Web, and a question and answer facility with "Dr Risk" about pricing, risk management, trading and other derivatives subjects.

Options and Futures

Perhaps you are starting to look for some gearing to your investments in order to realise bigger gains. Or perhaps you are a financial director looking for some tools to manage your financial risk. With these sites, you should find enough to keep you happy.

LIFFE

www.liffe.com

> Overall rating - *****
> Speed - Fast
> Advertising Level - Low
> Free but pay for live prices

The web site for the hybrid exchange: London International Financial Futures and Options Exchange. On arrival you are given the choice between a Java or a non-Java site. If you have Windows 95 or above, then it is worth going for the Java option.

Inside you'll find details on all of the produces dealt on LIFFE with data pertaining to each future. There' a well stocked educational centre and a special section for private investors. If you are new to options and futures, then this should be one of your ports of call.

Other pages serve a glossary of Options and Futures, press releases and details of the inner workings of the exchange.

OptionsSource.com

OptionSource.Com
Preparing Investors for Success in Options Trading

www.optionsource.com

Overall rating - *****
Speed - Medium
Advertising Level - Low
Free

A great site for information. For the beginner there's a 'educational' area of the site containing details on getting started in Options which leads you through from the very basics to more advanced topics, explaining as you go. There are questions and answers (really and

FAQ file). For the more experienced Options investor, there's information on Options research and details of forthcoming seminars, plus a book and video store.

The general resources include a daily commentary on the market with some good insight, direct option quotes (delayed), a symbol look-up script and an Options calendar.

Futures Guide

FUTURES GUIDE
CALL 877 650-4736 FOR A FREE STARTER KIT

MARKET HOTLINE
delivered daily to your inbox!

http://www.futuresguide.com/

Overall rating - **
Speed - V Slow
Advertising Level - Medium
Free, pay for Ezine

A digest focused on Futures and Options. A relatively small site in this field. Flicks rather too quickly between the simple and the complex for most visitors. One moment you are having a tutorial on Bull Call Spreads and the next you are getting hard details on calculating the price of an option. Overall, the experienced

investor will get more from this site than the
beginner and should be seen as an intermediate
educational resource.

Prophet Charts

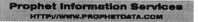

www.prophetcharts.com

Overall rating - *****
Speed - Fast
Advertising Level - Low
Free

Wow, why bother paying anyone for information when sites like this exist. This is a totally
free Java-based site which lives up to it's claim
to give you the 'most powerful charts anywhere

on the web'. You can get price and volume charts on any US listed stock (which includes most Blue Chips from around the world) or mutual fund, plus popular indices and futures charts.

But wait, it gets better. The Prophet Charts have features such as custom made trend lines, instant indicators and detachable windows for further analysis of the data. So, apart from receiving free historical data information, you are effectively getting a free analysis package!

If you are serious about Options or, indeed, any stock trading, visit this site.

How to place an Options order

http://www.gate.net/~bcharris/ordr.html

Overall rating - ****
Speed - Fast
Advertising Level - None
Free

A straight introduction on how to go about placing orders painlessly. If you don't want to get caught out by the jargon and the timing of your order, take a read of this page first.

New York Mercantile Exchange

www.nymex.com

New York Mercantile Exchange

NYMEX/COMEX. Two divisions, one marketplace

Overall rating - *
Speed - Fast
Advertising Level - None
Free

One of the poorer offering from Exchanges around the world. Contract specs, charts, delayed data and information about the Exchange, and one of the longest disclaimers ever fitted on a web page - that's about it. Occasionally you'll get scintillating details about forthcoming Coal Futures seminars. Come on NYMEX and COMEX, you can do better than this.

Options Analysis

www.optionsanalysis.com

> Overall rating - ***
> Speed - Medium
> Advertising Level - Medium
> Free delayed prices

Straight into price information and ranking indicators for Stock Options and Futures Options. If you don't want to pay for the 'Platinum Site' with 'instant' prices, you can search for free intraday delayed prices by stock or index symbol.

Perhaps the best part of this site, though, is the excellent links page. Here you'll find a well categorised series of Futures and Options links. Those which stand out are the gurus in this field with mini-biographies and links to their published material.

Chicago Mercantile Exchange

www.cme.com

> Overall rating - ***
> Speed - Fast
> Advertising Level - None
> Free

Details of what's traded, such as contract sizes and specifications, on CMEX with delayed prices. Some information is given on how to get started in Futures and Options plus links to educational resources as well as those published by the exchange itself. A 'Trader's Corner ' could give you an inside line oh what's hot, but is more likely to let you know about trader's senses of humour than anything else.

Chicago Board of Trade

www.cbot.com

Overall rating - ****
Speed - Fast
Advertising Level - None
Free

The main unique point of this site has to be the mock trading function which you can run online. How would you hack it as an online

Futures and Options trader? Fancy your chances? Then give it a try here before you go live with your hard earned wages.

Another good point of CBOT is that it puts up free live charts rather than being delayed. If all the other exchanges follow this example, then online dealing will become a real possibility for everyone, rather than the privileged few. On top of everything, you will find trading software, strategies and updates. Everything else is generated for members (and 'no' you can't join online), such as Exchange funded research results.

Internet Banking
The Way Forward?

Internet banking certainly should be the future. The whole system of making payments, checking accounts and transferring money fits so superbly into modern technology it is hard to know why we aren't all banking on the Internet already. Well the answer, of course, lies with the banks themselves.

Only around one third of the largest banks offer any form of on-line banking. And you can guess why the other two thirds are slow on the up take. It is because they cannot see any way of making money from you, the customer, in the short term.

Also, banks are not exactly known for their gung-ho approach to life, and they are all busily hiding in the shadows waiting for one of their competitors to show them the way before they jump in with both feet and try to catch up.

Accountancy firm Ernst & Young have produced a report showing that 96% of banks don't think the Internet will help them gain any extra customers or generate new income streams. Instead they seem to view the opportunity merely as a way of saving money and dropping their transaction costs.

Sooner or later, however, one of the banks is going to pick up the baton and run with it. They are going to show the others how it is done and have new customers flocking to their doors. And then, in an instant, all the rest of the major banks will try to make out that they have been Internet savvy since the days of ARPA.

But that is enough cynicism. What are banks currently offering the on-line investor. Those who are on-line, the trail blazers, sadly only offer even the simplest services. At present you can expect to get:

✔ The ability to check your account balance and find out what funds you have available.

✔ A facility for transferring money between accounts, certainly within the same bank and possibly between banks,

✔ Methods for paying bills,

✔ The ability to pay standing orders and

✔ An ability to export your own financial data to your PC so you can analyse it using other software.

On-line banking in this form is generally safe (through the use of encryption) extremely convenient since you can do it at any time that suits yourself and less time consuming than any other methods of banking (no parking, no standing in line). However one major downside of Internet banking seems to be that they forbid you to interact with any of their employees.

If you go into the bank you get to talk to the clerks and even if you use telephone banking you are speaking to a real person. However Internet banks rarely give you the facility for e-mailing their staff since, presumably, they see this of a new source of workload and therefore cost.

Getting to a stage where you can have all this convenience on your desktop is fraught with a few difficulties.

Firstly opening an account on-line would seem an obvious thing to do. But only about one in five of the banks on the Internet will allow you to open an account directly over the net. And even those that do admit that calling them up on the phone will get the job done a lot quicker than using the on-line method.

Secondly when you do get your account open you will probably find that there are a lot of teething problems at the beginning. These may include connection problems, such as with passwords and details being entered incorrectly. They may also include electronic payments that don't get processed because something in the account set up isn't quite correct. You may even find that the same bill may be paid twice or money transferred between accounts on two occasions because a button has accidentally been pressed twice or the bank's computer has seen fit to read the same instructions two times over. (While we are talking about problems with opening accounts it is probably worth mentioning that very few on-line banks describe their exact fee structure and minimum balance requirements for opening and running an Internet based account).

The Internet stretches around the globe so you now have the ability to open a bank account in any country around the world and to take advantage of their financial facilities such as lower interest rates to arrange cheaper mortgages - NOT!

US banks will only open accounts for US residents and the same can be said for British banks. Even though the technology

---

exists and security procedures can be put in place the banks just don't seem capable of dealing with foreigners (shock). Given that you are restricted to opening an Internet account with a bank in your own country here are a few questions that you should be asking:

- ❏ What fees are associated with your Internet banking account?
- ❏ How long does it take the transactions to be acted upon?
- ❏ Are transferred funds paid in available immediately?
- ❏ What steps do the bank take to correct errors that may occur?
- ❏ Have the bank experienced any on-line security failures? (And be suspicious if they don't own up to anything even when pushed).

And finally,

- ❏ How difficult is it to close the account if you are not satisfied?

Good luck, and don't forget to get contact details for a real live person for when things go horribly wrong ;-)

Banks

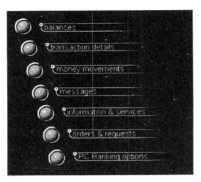

balances

transaction details

money movements

messages

information & services

orders & requests

PC Banking options

First Direct

www.firstdirect.co.uk

Overall rating - **
Speed - Slow
Advertising Level - None
Free

This facility is created by First Direct the telephone banking arm of HSBC. It has been a long time in development and still isn't a "real" Internet banking facility.

The software is largely Java based which slows the site down quite badly. You can move money between your account and display a transaction breakdown from one account at a time. You can make payments from your account while you are on line but only to destinations that you have already given to the bank over the phone and for all of those who like to see how the banks make their money from us you can check your bank charges on line.

One of the pluses of the site is that you can download the previous four months worth of your accounts data in a good selection of file formats for you to analyse off line.

Citibank

www.citibank.co.uk

Overall rating - ***
Speed - Medium
Advertising Level - None
Free

Citibank is one of the worlds best known banks with a presence in over 100 countries. So it is not surprising that they have embraced the Internet. The range of services offered includes the ability to view your account balances, details of transactions and to transfer money

between Citibank and another bank in the same country or to another customer at the same bank.

You can pay and cancel your bills on line as well as setting up and cancelling standing orders. All figures are shown in real time and you can view up to 90 days worth of transactions when you log on.

The main downside to having an account at this bank is that you have to maintain a balance of £2,000 and to make at least one transaction per month through the Internet banking service.

So if you are not ready to truly embrace into Internet banking you would be better looking elsewhere. If on the other hand you are ready to give it a go straight away this would be a reasonable choice.

Barclays

www.ibank.barclays.co.uk

Overall rating - **
Speed - Slow
Advertising Level - None
Pay

This site shows an impressive set of facilities but the bank itself takes time implementing what you ask it to do. The site is Java based which slows it down unnecessarily. You can view previous transactions and transfer funds between the various Barclays account.

However you can only receive a disappointing six weeks worth of data while you are online - disappointing when it is a pay for service. If you also have a Barclaycard you will find that you are able to pay your bill while you are online.

Co-operative Bank

www.cooperativebank.co.uk

Overall rating - ***
Speed - Slow
Advertising Level - None
Free

Another Java based system and this time with a massive applet which takes ages to download. Once into the bank you can check the state of your current account but you can only view the transactions you have made since you were last sent a printed statement.

You can pay bills to other accounts but again these have to be to other accounts that have already been agreed with the Co-op over the phone. you cannot export your action data to any files for analysis off line which is a bit of a pain and although you can order new cheque books and paying in books over the net this really does not compensate.

Bank of America

www.bofa.com

> Overall rating - ***
> Speed - Fast
> Advertising Level - None
> Pay (Free under conditions)

A very user friendly interface for a bank that is making a real effort on the Internet. You will have to pay for the services unless you agree to have your pay cheque deposited direct into your account.

On the plus side, however, you don't need to keep a minimum deposit in your account to continue using the facilities. The site offers a great deal more than the standard banking facilities and you will find details of seminars to help you handle your money and a "money tip of the day". If you are into hire things you can check the corporate goings on at Bank of America and their views on the economic situation on the company.

Security First Network Bank

www.sfnb.com

Overall rating - ****
Speed - Medium
Advertising Level - None
Free

A slightly complex interface but probably the best bank on the Internet at present. If you are still not sure about on line banking you might want to pop along to this site and view SFNB's on line banking services demonstration. If you are still impressed then you can take a second tour around the bank this time with a few more details thrown in.

A tutorial that comes along with the tour shows you the type of transactions that you are allowed to make if you sue the bank on line. The list of products is quite impressive and all of the services are fee if you maintain the minimum $100 deposit. Data can be exported to the major software manufacturers packages for analysis off line and this is one of the few banks that encourage you to interact with it.

Wells Fargo

wellsfargo.com

Overall rating - ****
Speed - Medium
Advertising Level - None
Pay

This is another bank that has made an effort to make their interface friendly and easy to use. There are plenty of facilities at this bank but you will have to pay for it an keep a minimum balance in our account.

You have got the basic tools that you associate with an on line bank such as checking your balances, your transactions and paying bills over the Internet to pre-arranged accounts but Wells Fargo like to throw in some extras.

Apart from news tickers you will find some lighter content such as happenings on "this date in history", ways of protecting your computer from virus' and special deals that Wells Fargo has managed to forge with other companies. This is somewhat of a novelty. A bank trying to entertain you while they take your money, whatever next?

Currencies

The world is becoming a smaller place al most day-by-day, helped immensely by the Internet. But the days of an international currency are a long way off yet, despite the best efforts of some European countries with the euro. Until then, you can keep track of fluctuations, and play at being George Soros with some of these sites:

Information.Internet

www.info-int.com

Overall rating - *
Speed - Medium
Advertising Level - None
Free

Information Internet are the developers of MarketMaker which is a real-time financial dealing system for the Internet. Foreign exchange prices can be found using this proprietary windows program along with graphical indicators of currency movements.

This is top end software which is addressed to the issues of security, speed, reliability and maintenance.

INO Global Markets

exchanges.quotewatch.com/exchanges/forex.html

Overall rating - ***
Speed - Fast
Advertising Level - Low
Free basics, pay for full service

Provides 24 hour quotes and charts on all major and second line currencies around the world. The charts and quotes page presents the opening, the high and low price, the last price, the change and the time it was updated for each currency. To see further information such as specific charts, options and the latest headlines for each currency you simply click on the link. The same site also includes data on many other futures and options.

OANDA

www.oanda.com

Overall rating - ****
Speed - Medium
Advertising Level - Low
Free with registration

A site run by Olsen & Associates with historical tables, current rates and forecasts for all of the worlds major currencies. Registration to the site is free and that gives you access to some quite heavyweight information.

At the lower end you have some simple newsflashes and a currency converter and at the top end you have advanced currency forecasts showing the most likely future directions and prices and comments to help you with your currency investments.

If you like to make your own decisions you will find an over bought/over sold summary, a currency ranking analysis chart and a downloadable historical exchange rate final plus many currency related research papers.

Fraud on the Internet

Rapid expansion of the Internet in such an unregulated manner and the speed at which new possibilities are being discovered has caused many industry observers to liken cyberspace to the Wild West.

In many respects, and particularly when it comes to investment, this is an accurate description. Whilst most of those taking part are law abiding citizens the Internet has attracted it's fair share of carpet-baggers, swindlers and fraudsters.

These unscrupulous con merchants realise that not everybody on the Internet are totally familiar with how things work. So they seek to take advantage with the fact that you are out of the world that you know and are comfortable with, and will hold you hand while they take you for a "ride" on the information super highway.

Until the law makers catch up with the speed of development that is embraced by the

Internet (or should we say "if") a larger slice of responsibility will have to fall on your own shoulders for looking after yourself. The cosy sentimental culture developed in this age of litigation where anybody can sue somebody else if anything goes wrong simply does not apply in cyberspace. In short, the Internet buyer better be very aware.

The Federal Trade Commission has estimated that **the average on-line fraud costs a victim around about $20,000 per incident**. Some of the schemes that have come to light have been for as little as a few thousand dollars but the largest that has been disclosed (and some major corporations probably don't want us to know that they have been taken for a ride) are for sums greater than half a million dollars.

Only a small amount of effort on your behalf will prevent you from becoming the next victim of the super highway robber. By far the most important rule that you can apply is not believe everything that you read. Any real story that you see on the Internet and any investment opportunity that you come across should be able to be cross referenced with at least two major sources. Of course it may just be that you've come across a fantastic opportunity that no one else has heard of but it is more than likely that something is amiss. Just as a technical analysts will wait for the market to turn before he or she invests heavily, perhaps should wait until a few more people are discussing a particular investment opportunity before you commit any cash.

Whilst you may not know how to do it yourself it is extremely easy to publish anything that you would like to onto the Internet. If you don't believe this try logging onto some of the more dubious sites that deal with illegal pornography and extremist political views. You will find lots of stuff published on these sites that you simply could not get away with in "real life".

The investment market is no different. Fraudsters can set up an impressive looking web site at a very low cost with just a little bit of knowledge. They can also e-mail huge numbers of people without any great personal investment. So the cost of entry into fraudulent activity are a lot lower on the Internet than they are anywhere else. Cyberspace also offers the swindlers the chance to appear and disappear in an instant. Once they disconnect themselves from the Internet they are simply "gone" and it is virtually impossible to track them down.

Don't think that you will be able to spot unscrupulous investment offers by their lack of professionalism. Apart from creating impressive web sites the serious fraudsters will post messages across many different Usenet groups and employ people to pick up and respond to questions in such a manner as to convince you that they are part of a large and reputable company.

You could think, for example, that you are checking out an investment opportunity that you have heard from person A in misc.invest with person B in news.admin.invest.futures. You may even exchange correspondence with person C in misc.invest.options.

If all of you agree that it is a good investment opportunity should you then plough your money straight into the stock? After all, you weren't to know that person A, B and C were the same person logged on under different e-mail addresses were you?

Danger Signs

Given that on-line fraudsters can act in a very professional manner, and convince even the most astute investor that an opportunity is waiting for them, how can you tell what is good and what is bad. The answer lies in the manner in which they operate. Scanners will:

Always offer exceptionally high profits. These are designed to get your interest and make you salivate at the potential zeros on your bank balance. If profits look too good to be true they probably are and you are likely to end up with just the one zero in your bank account.

Offer very high returns with a low perceived risk. This just does not happen in the world of finance. The only investments that carry no risk at all are bonds and Gilts offered by governments of industrialised nations, anything else will carry a risk relative to those bonds. The greater the risk level the greater the return you can expect. If there were any way of making high returns with a low risk everyone would already be doing it.

Use pressure tactics. Any form of hard selling should be an immediate indicator.

"Special deals just for you" are the Internet equivalent of the old foot in the door.

Make you think time is running out. The longer you are given to think about something the less chance there is that you are going to be parted with your money. So Internet fraudsters will always make you think there is a reason for urgency. Sure you may miss a gem of an opportunity by not "getting in" straight away, but wouldn't you rather make just half of the potential profit and be sure that you are not going to kiss goodbye to your hard earned money?

Asking Questions

The National Futures Association recommends that asking questions is a good way of avoiding potential fraudsters. Dishonest dealers don't want you to think clearly and they are likely to bombard you with all forms of diversionary questions.

While you are thinking the answers through they are firing another question at you and slowly turning you around into their direction. If this happens and you are becoming suspicious of a situation turn the tables and start asking the questions yourself.

Here are four questions that should route out the majority of unscrupulous brokers:

● **Where did you get my name?**

If you receive an answer such as a "select list" or you were specially selected from a list of clever investors, or something simpler like a newsgroup members list you should start to be suspicious. An honest broker should have no qualms of about letting you know where they got their leads.

● **What are the risks involved with the recommended investment?**

A dishonest sales person will talk down the risks involved and try to make you think you are investing in the safest thing ever to hit the market. An honest broker will give you a direct answer and should use some form of benchmark against which they are measuring the risk involved in the investment.

● **What regulatory agency do you belong to and which investment body looks after the product?**

No fraudulent salesman wants you going to any regulatory body to check on them or the investments they are trying to sell. Obviously if you did so the body is unlikely to have heard of them or the investment, and if they have, it will probably be negative.

Can I have your advice in writing?

A double sucker punch to the potential fraudster. First of all they will try and get your money immediately so that they will claim that there is no time to send you their details. Secondly there is no way that they want to give you written evidence that could at some time turn up in court. Remember that these guys only exist for a fleeting moment on the Internet while they make their killings and disappear. Leaving evidence around is not their trademark.

Lock Your Doors

There has been a great deal of discussion on the web about security issues, and in particular giving out your credit card details and bank account number. A lot of this information, or should we call it dis-information, has been coming direct from companies and corporations that have an interest in creating a general air of fear.

Check the source behind any scare story and you will probably find that it is a company that makes encryption programmes or has a new way of handling electronic cash transactions. All the time we are being bombarded with horror stories of about how hackers can snatch sensitive information such as credit card details direct from the Internet and empty your bank account while you are sleeping.

Indeed to listen to some of the stories you would think that the mere act of going on-line will mean you losing your house, having your identity completely blanked out and your grandmother's maiden name being changed by deed poll!

But how many times have you seen interviews or heard from the people that this has happened to? Most of these stories are just that - stories - and no more than technical possibilities.

This security hysteria has resulted in rapid growth for businesses to offer secure transaction processing. Encryption companies who deal with password software have suddenly made a small fortune. Browsers security has been pushed to the front by Microsoft and Netscape who have been quick to pay multi-millions of dollars for software companies specialising in this area. Obviously the scare stories have worked.

Thankfully time is proving to be a great healer in this respect. Masses of new people join the Internet every day and slowly people are beginning to realise that they are not being ripped off at every corner. It may start with a simple purchase of a book from Amazon.com but once people realise that they can give their credit card details and they won't be misused everyone will become happier with financial transactions over the Internet.

The knowledge and technology required to intercept credit card details via package sniffers or any other form of Internet wizardry is far too difficult for the common crook. It is far, far easier for them to look over your shoulder when you make a purchase in a store and write down the details of your card directly.

You will also be interested to know that nearly two thirds of credit card fraud is perpetrated by those who are suppose to receive your credit card details - such as sales assistants in major stores.

Now, are you sure you locked that back door?

SEC

www.sec.gov

U.S. SECURITIES AND EXCHANGE COMMISSION

A US regulatory agency with responsibility for protecting investors in the securities markets. The Commission also regulates firms engaged in the purchase or sale of securities, people who provide investment advice, and investment companies.

Notcon.com

notcom.com

An Internet anti-fraud initiative for the UK financial services industry. Provides up-to-date information about Internet frauds and top tips on how to avoid them.

Flare

www.cs.ucl.ac.uk/research/flare/

A DTi funded project for the prevention of fraud where the problem or solution is particularly associated with the use of technology.

Bookstores & Software

The huge online bookstores like Amazon.com probably stock, or can get hold of, every investment book you'd ever want. But searching through such huge stores is inconvenient, and since it isn't their speciality the running comments are almost non-existent.

Far better are specialist financial bookstores where their entire stock is completely cross-categorised and available for immediate shipping.

The software market is almost completely tied up by the Microsoft giant and Intuit. There are, however, several versions within each company's offerings, so take a look at the sites before buying to make sure you are getting the best for you.

Bulls & Bears Bookshop

www.global-investor.com/bulls-bears/

Overall rating - *****
Speed - Fast
Advertising Level - None
Free

Possible the best bookshop on the entire web. It stocks over 1,300 titles for immediate despatch, a real gain over the likes of Amazon.com if you need it really urgently - also their shipping costs are lower. There are plenty of special offers available and you'll find up to 20% off the books you want. All titles are cross referenced and you are able to search the site or browse through more than 50 categories.

Intuit

www.intuit.com

Best known for its lead product - Quicken - but also includes less well-known programs such as TurboTax and Tax Estimator for the American market. You can download a trial version of quicken after reading all about its functions and capabilities. You can also jump to the Quicken.com financial network, receive news stories and download historical data.

Microsoft Money

www.microsoft.com/money

The behemoth turned its attention to personal finance software and the predictable domination of the market was only held back by Intuits innovation. Whatever your thoughts on

Microsoft, their products are good and Money is no exception. It now comes as a stand alone or as part of the Money Suite or the Money personal & Business suite. You can download trial versions and receive up to $50 in rebate coupons for purchasing the full product.

In addition to product details, you'll find here Wall Street Journal headlines, financial FAQs, links to financial institutions and MSN MoneyCentral.

TTL

www.bookshopcentral.co.uk/Fbooks.htm

Overall rating - ****
Speed - Medium
Advertising Level - None
Free

Part of the much bigger Bookshop Central site which brings together specialist and general bookshops from around the web. TTL specialise in publishing easy-to-read introductions to subjects and is associated with Net.Works (publishers of this book)

Their best selling title is *Understand Derivatives in a Day* which is into it's fourth printing of the second edition, so it really must be possible to comprehend such a difficult subject quickly. Books are available on derivatives, shares, bands and gilts, commodities, financial risk, swaps, timing the financial markets (technical analysis) and several personal finance books.

Bonds

A bond is a promise from a company or institutuion to pay a lender of money a fixed sum of interest on a regular basis for a stated period. At the end of this period the loan, or principal, is repaid.

Such bonds are issued by the whole range of organisations including governments (national, provincial and municipal) and corporations. To the outsider it may look simple, but investing in bonds is a complex matter - as anyone who has attempted to calculate yield to maturity will testify.

The following Internet resources provide valuable information for all levels of bond investor including basic guides, prices, calculations and making choices.

Bloomberg Website

www.bloomberg.com/markets/uk.html

Overall rating - ****
Speed - Fast
Advertising Level - low
Free

Part of the much bigger Bloomberg site, this area presents price information and yeild curves for UK Government Gilts. From the same page you can access similar data for Canadian, French, German, Italian, Japanese and US Government bonds. Use the frame on the left to access other Bloomberg information, including yield curves for Municipal bonds.

Bank of England

www.bankofengland.co.uk

Overall rating - *
Speed - Fast
Advertising Level - None
Free

Information is the name of the game here. Sadly it is presented with little imagination

and limited to those very official press releases.

Nevertheless, it is the information which comes out of this organisation which has a bearing on the performance of UK Gilts, so it is worth dropping by every so often for the detail behind the stories you'll have heard leaked out on the news!

Her Majesty's Treasury

www.hm-treasury.gov.uk

> Overall rating - **
> Speed - Fast
> Advertising Level - None
> Free

Another source of information for UK Gilt investors. A slight improvement on the bank of England, but again it isn't going to win any innovation awards. Find official copies of those leaked Government documents on the health of the economy, and especially interest rates, government debt and the funding of new initiatives. Is there a new issue coming to market to fund the latest folly?

InvestingBonds.com

Investinginbonds.com

www. Investinginbonds.com

Overall rating - *****
Speed - Moderate
Advertising Level - Nil
Free

An excellent site for those who are new to investing in bonds as well as a useful resource for more experienced bond traders.

For the beginner there's seven simple steps to educating yourself about investing in bonds; including how much of your portfolio should be in bonds, an investors checklist, a basic guide to bonds and how to read bond prices in the newspapers. Finally, there's a free online version of their booklet explaining how inflation and interest rates affect bond prices.

For the experts check out information as diverse as daily municipal bond prices and advice on compound interest in relation to Zero Coupon Bonds.

Bonds Online

www.bonds-online.com
www.bondsonline.com

Overall rating - ***
Speed - Fast
Advertising Level - Medium
Free but pay for prices

A large site with plenty of information for everyone but mainly aimed at experienced bond investors with a bent towards the news angle. You will need to pay for most prices (provided by Reuters). On the site you'll find 'what's new' as well as bond market news. There's special pages for treasuries, municipals, savings bonds and corporates.

Welcome to.....

For those who want to keep abreast of developments there's information on the latest bond research. If you can't find what you want, there are questions and answers with the 'Bond Professor'. The associated online newsletter (pay) gives bond recommendations and special situation information.

Brady Net

www.bradynet.com

> Overall rating - ****
> Speed - Fast
> Advertising - Medium
> Free - basic
> Pro - Pay

A valuable source of information for everyone interested in bonds associated with Emerging Markets. Free information include the latest market commentaries, newslinks and discussions with a separate forum for each asset).

You can get a free 14 day trial of the BradyNet Pro Center which include the following features: live prices and intra-day charts, research and analysis, evaluations of the latest issues, custom made charts and a portfolio manager.

You can also download historical data and perform spread differential analysis. A useful feature of this site is the search facility offered on the opening page, with special options.

4Bonds.com

www.4bonds.com

> Overall rating - **
> Speed - Medium
> Advertising Level - Medium
> Free

Part of the 4Internet Network, this site is an initial list of links which are directly or indirectly related to bonds and bond trading. Lists of brokers and dealers, software and products, financial news, information and resources and stock quotes can be expanded to give more choices.

US Savings Bonds Online

www.publicdebt.treas.gov/sav/sav.htm

A Fairly basic site giving reasons for buying bonds, the types of savings bonds you can buy and a free calculator of how much they are worth. Navigating the site is not the easiest with numerous drop-down boxes and far too many choices for a logical progression. Once you do locate the information you want on Savings Bonds, it is detailed and useful, so it's worth persisting if you have a special interest in this area.

The Blue List

www.bluelist.com

A division of McGraw Hill, this site is the online version of a printed publication concentrating on listing current bond offerings from municipal government departments and corporations. Free information is limited to supplementary commentary and some forecasts as well as the less useful info on what's new in the bond world, history of the Blue List and links to Standard and Poor's web sites.

```
Overall rating - ***
Speed - Fast
Advertising Level - Low
Pay with limited free areas
```

If you wish to subscribe you get full access to the whole site, including up-to-the-minute par values, a blue List bond ticker service, an online daily publication and daily scans of the most recent offerings. Volumes are a good indication of the market and you can view the most actively traded bonds amongst dealers and brokers, with a full daily summary of trades.

JP Morgan

www.jpmorgan.com/MarketDAtaInd/
GovernBondIndex/

The JP Morgan Government Bond Index is the most widely used benchmark for measuring bond performance and for quantifying risk across international fixed income bond markets.

The indices measure the total, principal, and interest returns in each market and can be reported in 19 different currencies. By including only traded issues open to international investors, the Index provides a realistic online measure of market performance.

Moody's Investor Services

www.moodys.com

Free but pay for prices. One of the main bond institutions, and an institutional website to

match. There's very little here of use to most investors. Indeed the site appears to have been built to please the bosses rather than to be a resource for investors.

Dreadful design sees constant 'symmetric' use of buttons on each side of a linked phrase, and an overuse of centred fonts. If you love little graphical button, though, you'll like it.

Brokers On-line

The Good The Bad and The Ugly

Trading direct over the Internet is now a reality. And with just over 40% of all deals brokered in the US taking place over the web it looks as if the future of brokering certainly lies in cyberspace. This can only be a good thing for the average person in the street as it democratises the equity markets and gives every one an equal chance to live and die by their own decisions.

There are three types of brokers that you can find on the Internet. They may not be the good, the bad and the ugly but they are full service brokers, discount brokers and deep-discount brokers.

The service that you can expect from each is vastly different. Full service brokers will give you advice on the stocks that you are buying including a potted history and details of how prices have been moving. They will also give you their opinion on whether you are making a good move or a bad one. Deep-discount brokers on the other hand will do nothing other than execute your requests. 'Discount broker' is a catch all term which refers to brokers who fall somewhere in between these two extremes.

If you think that this is the way you would like to go with your own dealings the first thing you need to do is check out a list of prospective brokers. You can use the ones reviewed in investing on the Internet or discover your own through the use of search engines and recommendations from newsgroups.

But however you go about finding your broker it is essential that you make enquiries as to their pedigree. In short you need to check with the regulatory authorities to make sure they are who they say you are and they don't have any black marks against their name.

All reputable brokers will be a member of one association or another and those associations should be able to give references if required. The short cut to finding out this source of information is to visit the brokers sites where, if they have got any marketing skills whatsoever, they will tell you about their membership to any such organisation. After all if they have honed their services to a level where an association will admit them as members then they will want to brag about it, won't they?

The next step is to investigate the differences between the services which each broker offers. You already know about the differences between deep-discount brokers and full service brokers but are there any value-added services that the broker offers such as free real time stock prices?

Here are a few features that you can tick off as you look over their web site:

- ✔ Are you required to keep a minimum amount in your account?

- ✔ Is there a monthly fee for keeping your facility with the company?

- ✔ Is it easy to get a cash balance for your account over the Internet?

- ✔ How will you be able to check on the status of any orders that you have placed?

- ✔ Are there any charges for postage of such confirmations or share certificates?

- ✔ Are confirmation messages sent out for your trades via e-mail, telephone or through the mail?
- ✔ Can you keep track of your portfolio value?
- ✔ Are you able to view or download a history of your transactions?

The Price is Right

As with traditional brokers you need to investigate the prices charged by Internet brokers very closely. This is not an easy task as every broker seems to have its own fee structure making direct comparisons very difficult.

One broker may for example charge a relatively high fee for executing orders but not require you to keep a significant minimum balance and at the same time providing you with free real time prices.

Another broker, on the other hand, could be charging a lower rate for execution of orders but require that you keep a high value in your account and charge you for the supply of real time data.

Different ways of charging include:
- A flat rate charge,
- An extra fee for limit orders,
- A fee per thousand shares,
- A different fee for market orders,
- One fee for transactions on a certain exchange and a different fee for transactions on another,
- A minimum fee, and
- A fee based on the percentage of the value of your transaction.

But however you come to your conclusions you will be pleasantly surprised to see how much cheaper it is to do your share transactions over the Internet.

Getting Going

Once you have researched which broker you would like to use on the Internet and decided that they offer the best service on a value-for-money basis it is time to open an account.

A few brokers will allow you to do this on-line but the majority still prefer to speak to you on the telephone. Which ever way they go about things you will be required to fill in a form and deposit a minimum amount of cash into your account. Expect the process to take two to three weeks in even in this day and age!

While you are waiting for the paperwork to take its course, now would be a good time for you to practice trading on-line before you use real money. If your chosen broker has a simulation facility then use this otherwise just go through the motions of placing an on-line order but omitting to click that all-important last button and abandoning your trade without ever sending it.

This will allow you to get use to specifying the details that are required by the broker, in particular specific stock symbols or "tickers". Get used, also, to entering the number of shares that you require and the correct units for currency. Remember it is you who is placing the order and if you enter a price which is an order of magnitude out you have only got yourself to blame for the consequences.

Another benefit of practising entering orders is to minimise the time it will take you when you need to place an urgent request. If a useful bulletin hits your PC via push technology, is it going to take you an hour to look up

the correct address of your on-line broker, locate the relevant company's ticker symbol,
check the balance of your account, and enter
the details before submitting your order? Or are
you going to be able to have your transaction in
the market within a couple of minutes? Lost
minutes floundering around in cyberspace can
mean the difference between a hefty profit and
a missed opportunity.

Don't worry too much, however. Once you
have gone through the rigmarole of setting up
your account and got your first transaction out
of your system you will wonder how you ever
did without an Internet broker.

When placing your order and calculating
the fees that will be attached to it you
will need to know the difference between
one type of order and another.

Market orders. A market order will be
executed by your broker at the best price
available at the time. They will not hold
onto the order for any time or seek a specific price.

Limit order. In this form of order you
will specify the top price that you are

willing to pay in the case of a purchase or the minimum price you will accept if you are selling. If these prices are not achievable then your order will not be executed.

Stop order. When the price reaches that set by a stop order then the order will become active and the transaction will take place. This only guarantees that the transaction will actually be executed and does not fix the price.

Stop-limit orders. This is like the combination of a stop order and a limit order. When a share price reaches a pre-determined price the order is activated. But with a stop-limit order this will be cancelled again if the maximum or minimum prices stated are not available.

Day order. A day order is only valid for the day on which it is placed. If it can not be executed within that date then it will be cancelled.

Good-till-cancelled. This form of order is exactly what it says. It remains in the market and can be executed at any time providing the agreed prices are achieved unless it is cancelled by the person who has placed the order in the first instance.

Brokers

Sharelink

www.sharelink.co.uk

Sharelink is part of the group of companies owned by the Charles Schwab Corporation. To-

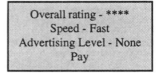

Overall rating - ****
Speed - Fast
Advertising Level - None
Pay

gether they have nearly 25 years of experience in the US and over 11 years in the UK. Combined, the corporation believes they have dealt for over five million investors.

The site offers dealing and safe custody service for shares, investment trust, unit trust, corporate bonds, Gilts, and cash. Dealt through an account denominated for either the US market or the UK market. Other services include real-time prices, in-depth news, research and analysis. And even though Sharelink are a discount broker you will find on-line personal assistance seven days a week.

Stocktrade

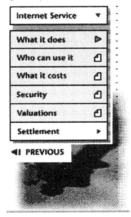

www.stocktrade.co.uk

> Overall rating - **
> Speed - Fast
> Advertising Level - None
> Pay

Stocktrade clients can ask for live, on-line dealing prices and then actually confirm and on-line instruction at the price they have been quoted. In other words clients are effectively not only able to receive live dealing prices on line but to deal with those exact prices.

The stock trade system copes with the entire settlement process. It deposits or takes delivery of shares from an electronic Crest account. It also ensures that once delivery has taken place

Internet Service	▼
What it does	▷
Who can use it	◁
What it costs	◁
Security	◁
Valuations	◁
Settlement	▶
◀ PREVIOUS	

payments are automatically actioned to or from your deposit account. Portfolio valuations and account balances of stocks or cash are also available on-line. The site is very simple and logical to use but the design could use an overhaul.

Lombard

www.lombard.com

Overall rating - ****
Speed - Medium
Advertising Level - None
Pay

One of the first US brokers to offer direct on-line trading, and has been voted best overall on-line broker for three years running.

When you open a Lombard account you get on-line trading of stocks, options, thousands of mutual funds, US treasury bills, notes, bonds and zeros at very competitive rates with no account maintenance fees. You also get access to top quality information including free unlimited real-time quotes and graphs, Zack's research and Reuter's news.

There is also a series of one to two page reports featuring investment research, stock valuation, analysis recommendations and much more. If any of the details in these reports change for any particular company you will be sent a real-time e-mail alert of the change and a recommendation for your action.

Fidelity Brokerage

www.fidelity.co.uk

Overall rating - ***
Speed - Medium
Advertising Level - None
Pay

Another international discount broker which offers more than just the ability to trade on line.

The site carries the latest market news and daily prices and it is up dated throughout the day.

Opening an account is very easy as is navigating the rest of the site. You will find guides to everything from global markets to tax free investing and comments on a range of topics from dealer activity to the outlook on international interest rates.

E*Trade

www.etrade.com

Overall rating - ****
Speed - Fast
Advertising Level - None
Pay

Another pioneer of the on-line trading business from the early days of the World Wide Web. Indeed E*Trade is fairly unique in that it is mostly Internet or computer based rather than being an extension of normal broking services. You will not be surprised to find, therefore, that most of the fees at this site are amongst the lowest you will ever find.

In addition to dealing there is a lot information such as what is happening in the markets, resources relating to stocks and options, mutual fund research and screening tools and a community for exchanging ideas with other E*Trade members. Other account benefits include real-time analysis reports and recommendations and associated activities such as the ability to re finance your mortgage.

Durlacher

www.durlacher.co.uk

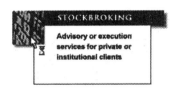

STOCKBROKING

Advisory or execution services for private or institutional clients

Overall rating - ***
Speed - Medium
Advertising - None
Pay

Specialises in high-tech stocks. The stock broking services on this site cover equities bonds and traded options. There is an overview of the markets and portfolio management included. Depending on which service you subscribe to you can access research reports and overviews of the various sectors.

There is newsletters that come with the recommend strategies and reports on all forms of investment on the Internet.

REDMAYNE BENTLEY

S T O C K B R O K E R S

Redmayne-Bentley

www.redmayne.co.uk/redmayne/start.htm

Overall rating - **
Speed - Medium
Advertising Level - None
Pay

The UK's first independent stock broker to get on the net. Redmayne-Bentley is amongst the largest of the independent stock brokers in the UK and could be described as offering an execution only service with add-ons.

Although you cannot invest directly on-line with this company you can find comprehensive details of their charges and their services from the execution only-plus service to the discretionary investments service. You will find market comment and an on-line version of their client's magazine Equity Insight.

Charles Stanley

www.charles-stanley.co.uk

Overall rating - ***
Speed - Medium
Advertising Level - None
Pay

This company offers a traditional advisory stock broking service and a dealing only service in addition to its fund management package. An array of financial information includes the latest FTSE 100 index level and a selection of the latest delayed London market prices.

CompuTEL Securities

www.computel.com

Overall rating - ***
Speed - Fast
Advertising Level - None
Pay

A division of Thomas F White & Co which offers on-line trading as well as real-time continuous quotes and news delivered direct to your desk top.

All accounts receive the free news service along with reports and insights needed to stay ahead on Wall Street. And if you subscribe to the premier accounts you get an e-mail signal service warning you of any changes.

If you are new to on-line trading you will find a very useful trading demonstration at the site which takes you through the whole process before you sign up or go live.

Killik & Co.

www.killik.co.uk

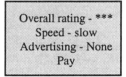

Overall rating - ***
Speed - slow
Advertising - None
Pay

This site is being upgraded to include on line trading facilities and additional research facilities. However at present it offers daily stock broking news which is free to everybody who visits the site. This is a handy daily market news column put together by Fleet Street's finest.

If you are registered as a Killik & Co client you will gain access to an impressive array of on-line research areas which are dotted around the site. The site is easy to navigate with drop down boxes and even includes a daily news search engine.

Calculators

Maybe you are a whiz at working out compound interest rates in your head, or a genius at spotting an arbitrage opportunity in the futures markets. But the chances are you still find things a lot easier with one of the many on-line financial calculators.

Financenter.com

www.financenter.com/calcs.html

Overall rating - *****
Speed - Fast
Advertising Level - Medium
Free

One of the most useful investment related sites that you will find anywhere on the Internet although it is a US site, even if you live elsewhere and invest your money in different countries you can use the huge number of calculators provided on this site to do your basic calculations by simply substituting

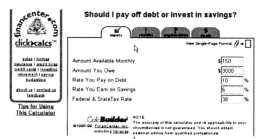

Should I pay off debt or invest in savings?

Inputs

View Single-Page Format

Amount Available Monthly	$150
Amount You Owe	$3000
Rate You Pay on Debt	10 %
Rate You Earn on Savings	6 %
Federal & StateTax Rate	38 %

NOTE
The accuracy of this calculator and its applicability to your circumstances is not guaranteed. You should obtain personal advice from qualified professionals.

your own currency (unless currency is involved in the calculation of course).

There are 12 categories from which you can choose to build a calculator. These include insurance, retirement planning, budgeting, credit cards, savings, stocks and bonds. Each one offers a drop down box and by clicking on the arrow to the right you can select from a longer list of different calculators.

For example, in the budgeting category you would click on the arrow to be given a list of possibilities one which may be "should I pay off debt or invest in savings?". You will then be presented with a calculator which asks for the amount of money available each month, the amount you owe, the rate you pay on your relevant debt, the rate you earn on your savings, and the prevailing tax rates.

Again the currencies are given in US dollars but they could quite easily be UK pounds, German Deutchmarks or even euros. Once your data is entered simply click on the results tab to see what comes up or another tab to get an explanation of the calculations.

BankAmerica

www.bankamerica.com/tools/sri_assetall.html

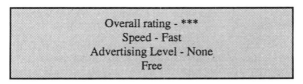

Overall rating - ***
Speed - Fast
Advertising Level - None
Free

This page provides you with a survey which when completed will suggest an investment strategy suitable for your current needs and your relevant situation.

You will find a description of the asset allocation strategy that you should adopt and indications as to how often you should review your objectives. You will find that you are able to clarify your thoughts and probably confirm to yourself what you should be doing by using this calculator.

Universal Currency Converter

www.xe.net/currency

Overall rating - ****
Speed - Fast
Advertising Level - Low
Free

A simple to use site which allows you to convert any amount of one currency into another. Since you are able to select the base currency and the currency that you are converting into it is easy to become confused as to which way you are performing the calculation so that the results handily include acronyms for the relevant countries.

If you are so inclined, you are able to include the universal currency converter on your own site which is very helpful for anybody who may have overseas sales.

Exchanges

This section covers some of the world's more important stock exchanges. The variation in quality of site is eye-opening with a few appearing to resemble a personal homepage than a professional website. When you get to some of the smaller exchanges the URLs also have a less-than-reliable feel about them.

In addition to the Exchanges themselves, we've covered exchange-related sites and those which offer services associated with them. You'll probably find this a rather 'dry' area compared to other investment areas on the web, but it's worth knowing a little about the organisations that help the world's money go around.

London Stock Exchange

www.londonstockex.co.uk

Overall rating - ***
Speed - Medium
Advertising Level - Low
Free

London STOCK EXCHANGE

The official site of one of the world's top three exchanges in the worlds leading exchange for international business. This web site tells you how the exchange in it's markets work and how to get in touch with the various people in their departments.

This is a great site if you ever really wanted to know what goes on in an exchange. There is a whole section which deals with using the stock market, what you get from it and how it works.

About the Exchange

Our Markets

News & Info

Using the Stock Market

There is also a comprehensive news and information service which will keep you informed of any changes. All of the markets that trade at the London Stock Exchange are comprehensively explained and there is a useful glossary of the terms used on an exchange.

FTSE

www.ftse.com

Overall rating - **
Speed - Fast
Advertising Level - None
Free but pay for special services

Not really an exchange as such but very closely related. The Financial Times Stock Exchange site gives you everything you need to know about the indices calculated by the company.

You will find all you need to know about the FTSE indices including how they are constructed and calculated. You will find recent end of day information including values from FTSE indices and you will be able to search the index database for constituents of the various indices, sectors and individual companies.

There is a news area which covers the latest news from the FTSE covering recent developments and index announcements. This is handy if you want to know which companies may be joining a particular index or dropping out.

This site also encourages feedback and you will find a FTSE forum where you can pose questions to the thousands of people who use the site as well as the Sysops who offer professional opinion. A range of special and consulting services are available through the site but these are probably only of use to top league investors.

SETS

www.sets.co.uk

```
Overall rating - **
Speed - Fast
Advertising Level - None
Free
```

This site is really part of the much larger London Stock Exchange Site but it is of particular interest to anyone who has suffered at the hands of this new order driven trading service.

A visit to this site will give you enough information to really understand how SETS work. And, if you haven't already done so, it will make your mind up to never place an "at best" order ever again. You will only find documentation relating to SETS at this URL but it is a great resource if you subscribe to the maxim "know thy enemy".

Crest

www.crestco.co.uk

Overall rating - **
Speed - Medium
Advertising Level - None
Free

CREST is the real time settlement for UK and Irish shares and other securities. It has taken over the settlement infrastructure for the UK governments bonds (gilts) and money market instruments and covers a wide range of settlement facilities.

The site is essentially a corporate show piece and it certainly covers everything there is to know about the CREST and the services it offers. But if you come here hoping to learn more about the settlement process you will be disappointed. It is more concerned with the politics of the situations such as the dawning of the euro and the Y2K problem.

You will find plenty of news releases, system proposals and operational faxes on this site and they make fantastic reading if you have trouble getting to sleep at night. You will get the idea of who they are trying to impress when you see the phrases "ready for the year 2000", "security of the system", and "improved and developed" are highlighted in red.

New York Stock Exchange

www.nyse.com

Overall rating - ****
Speed - Fast
Advertising Level - None
Free

A good site that fully deserves its four stars. You will find plenty of information and general news release relating to the NYSE as well as more information than you can every digest about the various markets that are traded there. There is also a comprehensive database of listed companies with associated links. Unlike its British counterparts this site does look beyond its own shores and has set aside an international view area on the site.

Realising that not everybody is an investment guru the NYSE has taken the effort to create and education resource on the site which is extremely useful for beginners and act as a good aide-memoire for the more experienced. For those who are interest in security of the whole system you can tap into details about market regulation. Finally the NYSE runs its own merchandise store so you can turn yourself into a walking advertisement for the exchange.

NASDAQ

www.nasdaq.com

Overall rating - *****
Speed - Fast
Advertising Level - None
Free but pay for special services

Just look at those stars! NASDAQ really has embraced the Internet and can be held up as a shinning example of how it should be done. They are streets ahead of the other exchanges and can safely compete with any other site on the Internet. The best place to start at this site is at the overview and then take a look at the site map. Indeed I would thoroughly recommend that you use the site map as your starting point when exploring the site so that you can use it as a jumping off location.

The other alternative would be to take the site tour but then you will find yourself locked into somebody else's opinion of the route that you should take. Here is just a sample of what you will find on the site. Portfolio tracking certainly compares with the commercially available services and if you have a portfolio of American stocks you will find it up there with the best. In the news section you will find specific market related releases and up to date company news.

Moving onto investor resources it is strange to see an exchange is giving you investment tips and strategies. There is an on line investment lesson and you can practice your skills with the best market simulation software that you will find on the Web. If you cannot find the resources that you are directly after why not pop along to the other "on line resources".

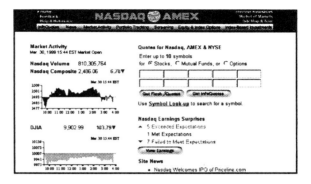

The equally impressive reference library will give you links to the other markets that are on line, a glossary of market and investment related terms, and links to academic institutions. There is also news about what is happening with the site and a market alert facility. A very comprehensive FAQ file appears in the help area but due to its usefulness it could quite easily be categorised as reference or resources. Also in the help area you will find more information about the site.

Back at the markets, and yes this is an exchange site, you will find details of market activity with movement of the major indices and breakdowns of the top movers by share volume, dollar volume, and percentage of advance or decline. There is comprehensive market statistics and a summary of tables relating to the exchange. All in all an excellent site.

Appearing in the market of markets area is lots of more information that really should be classified as reference. You will find well written articles on how stock markets differ, market characteristics, what investors want from a market, the evolution of NASDAQ, how orders are handled and executed and the way in which quotes are developed.

Associated NASDAQ Sites

NASDAQ - UK
www.nasdaq-uk.com/

NASDAQ Trader
www.nasdaqtrader.com
News coverage of exchange stocks. Features comprehensive trading volume reports.

NASDAQ News
www.nasdaqnews.com
Includes the latest Nasdaq Market press releases, statistics, IPOs, and other market information

Tokyo Stock Exchange

www.tse.or.jp

Overall rating - ***
Speed - Medium
Advertising Level - None
Free

A decent effort from the Tokyo Stock Exchange which can be extremely challenging if you choose the Japanese language option. You will find all the usual information about the exchange, listings, trading, clearing and settlement and details for getting listed on the exchange if you are a foreign company.

Apart from the news that affects the exchange you will find some hard information by way of stock prices and indices which historical charts and tables of prices. You will find relevant market data which combined with the index information will be extremely useful if you play the options market.

There is plenty of links on this site to listing companies, member firms and other financial institutions. Overall this is a good site for starting at if you want to investigate the Japanese and far east markets.

Mongolian Stock Exchange

www.mse.com.mn

Overall rating - **
Speed - Slow
Advertising Level - None
Free

Mongolian Stock Exchange. A surprisingly compact and useful site if you've ever wondered what goes on in the farther reaches of the world. There is an introduction to the Mongolian Stock Exchange with details presented very early on how the markets are regulated.

The trading system employed at the exchange is clearly explained with details of how clearing, settlement and depository systems function. Should you be wishing to join there is details of the stock exchange membership conditions and requirements and a chronicle of facts for anyone that wants to excel at trivia quizzes.

Frankfurter Wertpapierbörse

www.exchange.de

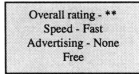

Overall rating - **
Speed - Fast
Advertising - None
Free

Deutsche
Börse

A rather dry but efficient site from the largest German Stock Exchange. The main features of this site centre around a description of the FWB its structure and its history.

Profiles and organisation structures seem to be the name of the game. There is a few details of indices and products with details of trading systems centre around the usual mission statement rubbish. You can get direct links from the same page straight to EurexDeutshland and Deutsche Borse AG.

Yahoo Directory of Exchanges

dir.yahoo.com/Business_and_Economy/ Finance_and_Investment/Exchanges/ Stock_Exchanges/

If you are after any more exchanges you'll find the biggest list at Yahoo. From Alberta to Zagreb and Amman to Winnipeg, there are links to more than seventy exchanges around the world.

www.nse.com.na

Top Internet Stocks

You Wished You had Bought first time around

So you know a lot about investing money on the Internet by the time you have reached this stage. But how much thought have you given to investing in Internet related stocks?

Sure we all know the story that the Internet is just a bubble in the market and that prices have gone far too high. Surely the rate of growth has been far too quick and the whole world of Internet related stocks is going to crash around their ears. But it just does not seem to happen.

If you go back onto the net and check out some historical news stories you will see that brokers have been predicting a fall in Internet related stocks for about the past three or four years. Yet the stories of rocketing stock prices continue to hit the screens.

EarthWeb is a typical example. It came to market in the midst of a lot of scare stories about over inflated Internet related stock prices. Indeed this sector had not increased for nearly a week! But on the first day of trading its shares tripled in value from $13 to $49. This despite the fact that the company only had net sales of $1.5 million and lost in excess of $12 million in the previous year.

Virtually all of the Super Highway stocks that have soared in value have done so against a background of heavy losses. It is easy, therefore, to make an argument that the Internet has had its day. But on the other side of the coin can you afford the financial risk of not being in a raging bull market?

Amazon.com is the one that everyone has heard of. Five years ago it did not exist and it owns and it still owns a grand total of zero high street shops. Yet the market capitalisation puts it ahead of major US book sellers such as Barnes & Noble and Borders. Sales show an almost exponential rate of growth but so do the associated losses. Nevertheless you cannot fail to admire a share growth of more than 400% from the work of just over 600 people.

Can this situation continue? The answer appears to be, "Yes" even though some managers from the industry don't really believe the situation themselves. In interview after interview directors claim that they know no reason for the stocks to continue climbing in the way that they are. Indeed one unnamed manager is known to have said that a corporation should not be able to exist at the rate they were losing money.

But don't take their word for it, look for yourself. Just take a random surf around the Internet and see how many times you see the company Amazon.com mentioned in one way or another and then look at the hits that those sites are receiving from like minded surfers around the world.

This is an awfully powerful brand awareness campaign and it is bound reap benefits. You can even check out the businesses yourself. From the comfort of your own room you can go along to Amazon.com and order a book to see how their services work. When the book arrives through the mail a few days later you will appreciate the benefits of doing business in cyberspace compared to a potentially fruitless trip into a mainstream book store.

Like them or loath them you need to think seriously about holding one or more if the following stocks in your portfolio.

America Online

This is one of the major players in the Internet service providers sector. Not only is it the owner of America Online itself but it has bought the CompuServe brand name and can boast one of the largest number of users connecting through its services.

It employs around 9,000 people and a typical return on your money over one year would be in excess of 250%. It is one of the few companies featured here to be able to show a profit on its recent balance sheet.

EarthWeb

The company which provides information resources for the information technology community primarily through its Developer.com web site. It is listed on the Nasdaq stock exchange and employs less than 100 people. Current losses dwarf their net sales.

Netscape Communications

The suppliers of software services for Internet users primarily known for their web browser. They are pioneers in their field and still hold a significant share of the browser market despite Microsoft's best efforts. They have also announced a tie in with other powerful companies such as America on-line.

Lycos

The company which develops on-line content and is positioning its well known search engine as a portal for web users. It is showing significant losses compared to its net sales but still this company of less than 500 employees shows total returns over one year of greater than 200%.

Excite

Like Lycos, Excite is best known for its on-line search engine. Despite making annual losses in the tens of millions since it was floated the telephone company A T & T paid $6.7 billion in one of the largest on-line 'mergers'. In one year you could have seen your investment increase by nearly 600%.

Doubleclick

This company develops advertising solutions for both purchasers and sellers of advertising space on the World Wide Web. The company is listed on Nasdaq and employs some 200 people but in the first year of listing the shares showed a six fold increase in value. At the same time losses more than tripled from $3 million to around $9 million.

eBay

This is an Internet auction house where anybody can buy and sell anything. With less than 100 employees it was listed on Nasdaq and in its first day of listing the shares rose five fold. At least this company has been able to report two years of operating profit!

Yahoo

Probably the best known search engine on the Internet and with some of the largest losses to boot. Like many others the company is yet to make a profit but has seen its share price soar. One year gain on investment would be over 550%.

Funds

Mutual funds, unit trusts, investments trusts, call them what you will, are heavily regulated in the US and UK. So it is not surprising that you will find little beyond basic fund information, prices and performance table on most of the following site - and even then preceded by a page or two of disclaimers. Nevertheless, the Internet offers plenty of information on funds which is easily accessible.

Quicken.com

www.quicken.com/investmetns/mutualfunds

> Overall rating - ****
> Speed - Fast
> Advertising Level - Medium
> Free

This is part of the much larger Quicken.com site. In the mutual funds section you will find lots of information that is worth reading before you invest. You will find mutual fund question

and answers, hot fund strategies and mutual fund fundamentals.

The site carries interviews with top fund managers and gives lots of views for the future as well as investment tips - although these are almost always showing some form of bias. The site features a "fund finder", the top 25 funds and drop down boxes which allows you to sort the funds by ranking over different periods such as 5 and 3 years.

CBS MarketWatch

www.cbs.marketwatch.com

Overall rating - ****
Speed - Fast
Advertising Level - Medium
Free

This site provides articles, news stories, and special features of interest to any mutual fund investor. You will find plenty of market data and research to help you choose where to put

 CBS MarketWatch
SuperStar Funds
Your Mutual Fund Center

 Sign up for your free
Kaufmann Investment Kit

which #1 fund?

your money. There is a comprehensive links page to fund sites for once you have made your decision.

For beginners there's a mutual fund tutorial and a chat room where you can find out more about fund investing. So the tools offered on the site include a portfolio builder, a fund tracker, a portfolio monitor, and a facility to see the funds that are requested most by the Internet investors.

Mutual Funds Online

www.mfmag.com

Overall rating - **
Speed - Medium
Advertising Level - Medium
Basic free with registration

This is the Web site of Mutual Fund magazine which has a pay for and free section. For the free section you will still need to register but you will receive access to free reports and newsletters, mutual fund hot links and dozens of other mutual fund tools.

Mutual Funds Channel

www.mutual-funchannel.com

> Overall rating - ***
> Speed - Fast
> Advertising Level - None
> Pay

This is a pay for site uses push technology to deliver, quotes, valuations, fund profiles, historical data, market analysis and market news to your desk top.

Instead of spending hours searching through the newspapers and talking to people on the telephone the idea is that you receive information on nearly 6,000 mutual funds delivered directly to your computer each day. So if you are an active mutual fund investor you will find this service extremely useful.

Interactive Investor

www.iii.co.uk/products/unit_trusts.htm

> Overall rating - ****
> Speed - Fast
> Advertising Level - Low
> Free

 **interactive** investor

This is part of the much larger III site and you will find separate sections specialising in unit trusts and investment trusts.

Essentially this is a group of sites from unit and investment trust providers all gathered together under one banner. The site offers current prices on over 15,000 investments and the performance histories on thousands of funds.

You are able to search fund news and browse through the relevant stories as well as join an inside discussion group. This site offers a great jumping off place for you to do your research before investing since you can access all of the leading product providers with just one click.

Elsewhere on this site you will find the Micropal Funds Performance page which covers all unit trusts, investments trusts and authorised off shore funds for the UK. It ranks individual funds for policies over 1, 3 and 5 years and gives comparisons for each fund for the sector average.

Trust Net

www.trustnet.co.uk

Overall rating - ****
Speed - Medium
Advertising Level - Medium
Free

This site covers more than 600 trusts and funds marketed in the UK. You will find trust profiles with performance charts, price history, and performance relative to the sector as well as details of capital structure and portfolio summary for each fund.

One of the better features on the site is the ability to rank the trust that you are interested in by performance (over 1, 3 and 5 years) and by discount to NAV. The same site also covers closed ended off shore and US funds.

Fidelity Investments

www.fid-intl.com

Overall rating - ***
Speed - Medium
Advertising Level - High
Free

the world of Fidelity

World's largest
independent investment
management organisation
& second largest discount stockbroker

This is the home site of the worlds largest independent investment management organisation and fund provider. From the home page you can access fund information for a number of regions including Europe (UK, France, Germany) and North America (USA, Canada).

Once you have worked your way down to the relevant fund you will find daily fund prices, regular market comments, as well as more general guides to fund investing and various interactive programs to help you with your investment decisions.

Cazenove & Co.

www.cazenove.co.uk

Cazenove & Co.
An overview of the firm

INSTITUTIONAL BROKING   CORPORATE FINANCE   FUND MANAGEMENT

Another of the large fund providers but a site that also includes lots of free web site resources. You will find UK sector performance tables which are up dated monthly as well as details on currency movements, major stock markets, short term interest rates and the bond markets.

Also mixed in with the main charts and prices of Cazenove unit trusts you will find information on the UK tax, the FTSE 100 constituent and a guide to global stock exchanges.

Financial Services

Fed up with pushy salesmen trying to sell you another insurance product you don't really want? Can't trust that supposedly independent financial advisor - you know, the one who always recommends his highest commission products? Want to make your own decisions and buy when you want to?

Then the Internet is the perfect place for you. No pressure, no race against time, and in the comfort of your own home, you can check out standard financial service industry offerings via the Web.

Insurance

Funny, isn't it, how your insurance policy covers you until something actually goes wrong, then everything is void. If you'd ever wondered why you have to ask four times for an insurance payout and go through endless rounds of letters for a simple transaction, take a look around the Web. Even if you are not looking for more insurance, you'll be amused by the length of the disclaimers on the sites.

The Chartered Insurance Institute
(UK)

www.cii.co.uk

Overall rating - *
Speed - Medium
Advertising Level - None
Free

Another site which is aimed at members. But yet again there is useful reading tucked away in corners. Use this site to find out if your insurer meets best practice levels and find out if they are a member of the institute. CII's generic insurance and financial services texts are recognised as world class reference works and can be searched for definitive technical data.

InsWeb
(US)

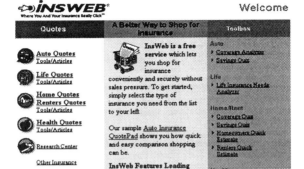

ww.insweb.com

Overall rating - ***
Speed - Fast
Advertising Level - Low
Free

A good site where you can shop for insurance conveniently and securely without the added sales pressure used by many 'live' salesmen. Simply follow the site tree by selecting options on each page, starting with Auto quotes, life quotes, home and renters quotes, and health quotes.

Apart from receiving a tailored quote, there's a toolbox of useful insurance-related goodies: savings quiz, homeowners quick estimate and a life insurance needs analyzer.

Association of British Insurers (UK)

www.abi.org.uk

Overall rating - *
Speed - Medium
Advertising Level - None
Free

Primarily for members of the association, but does include consumer advice and information. You'll find advice on a wide range of insurances including motor, holiday, home and contents, health, medical, life and pensions. This is worth looking at since it is independent of the actual insurance company.

Insurance News Network

(US)

www.insure.com

Overall rating - ***
Speed - Medium
Advertising Level - High
Free

Insurance related news and insurance features. This site includes several unique features such as an auto-theft forum where you can discuss car thieves, alarms, and other anti-theft devices.

Annuities
Auto
Business
Health
Homeowners
Life
Personal
In Your State
Company Ratings
Feature Stories
Insurance Toolbox
Help

There's another set of tools to help you calculate the amount of coverage you'll need in each category, and if you are so inclined, you can apply to receive the Insurance News Network newsletter.

Accountants

If you've got so much money you find it hard to keep track, or if your financial affairs are so complicated, you may need the help of an accountant. But then you wouldn't want to enlist the services of some of the sharks out there.

UK Accountants

www.uk-accountant.com

Overall rating - *
Speed - Fast
Advertising Level - None
Free

Follow your way through the pages by selecting the area of the country in which you live. When you've found the area, you can point at a map or select your locality to receive a somewhat small list of accountants. Each record includes an address, phone and fax number and the company's specialities.

American Accounting Association

(US)

www.rutgers.edu/Accounting/raw/aaa

Overall rating - *
Speed - Slow
Advertising Level - None
Free but pay for prices

The American Accounting Association promotes worldwide excellence in accounting education, research and practice - according to their mission statement, anyway.

That being the case, there are resources on the site which you may benefit from reading before you go along to your accountant and hand over your hard earned dollars. Apart from knowing the 'in-thing' as far as accounting goes, there's a useful links to accountants and other accounting organisations.

AICPA

(US)

www.aicpa.org

> Overall rating - ***
> Speed - Fast
> Advertising Level - None
> Free to access

The American Institute of Certified public Accountants site welcomes non members, particularly to the Tax Forum where all forms of topics come up, though it is moderated.

You will also find useful articles on topics such as taxation software reviews, taxation and students and tax newsflashes. It is possible to download IRS forms and publications and link to the Department of Revenue and Taxation. Perhaps the most useful function of the site is an Internet version of the Tax Information Phone Service (TIPS) where you can submit your questions via an online form.

Chartered Accountants Directory

(UK)

www.chartered-accountants.co.uk

> Overall rating - ***
> Speed - Fast
> Advertising Level - None
> Free

A much larger list and the accountants featured at this site are all chartered (the site appears to be developed by the Institutes of Chartered Accountants in England, Wales, Scotland and Ireland but is actually developed by a company called Datacomp).

A much wider selection of areas is available from this site and a there are many more accountants featured. If you are looking for a new accountant then this would make a very good starting place for your search.

Mortgages

Changing mortgage providers is becoming increasingly common with improved competition in the market place. These days it is definitely worth shopping around, and the potential saving from changing mortgages can outweigh the penalties for leaving your old scheme.

FT Quicken

(UK)

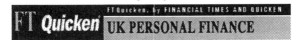

www.ftquicken.co.uk/planning

Overall rating - ***
Speed - Fast
Advertising Level - Medium
Free

Includes an excellent mortgage toolbox with many guides to help you understand your own needs in regard to mortgages. You can search for the day's best mortgage rates, calculate monthly repayments and find out if you could save money by remortgaging.

An online interactive MIRAS calculator will show you hoe much interest rate relief you'll receive each month. Site also carries mortgage news stories and press releases from mortgage providers.

Mortgage-Net (US)

www.Mortgage-Net.com

Overall rating - **
Speed - Medium
Advertising Level - High
Free

Read the top ten mistakes made by people who take out mortgages before you go any further. Then move on to read the mortgage FAQs and the mortgage calculators (plus other mortgage tools). If you are unsure about the type of mortgage you should be going for, you'll find advice in the interactive discussion forum and why not work things out for yourself with help from info on interest rate trends.

Infotrade Mortgage Service

(UK)

www.infotrade.co.uk/products/mortgage/mortg1.htm

> Overall rating - ***
> Speed - Slow
> Advertising Level - Low
> Free

More mortgage information and details of around 1,000 different mortgages from over 80 lenders. Includes assistence for CCJ's 100% mortgages, and high income multipliers.

Express Financial

(US)

www.efcol.com/calculators

> Overall rating - **
> Speed - Fast
> Advertising Level - Low
> Free

EXPRESS CALCULATORS

- Mortgage Payment Calculator
- Home Affordability Calculator
- Income Qualification Calculator
- Java Mortgage Calculator

Easy to use mortgage payment calculator, 'home affordability' calculator and income qualification calculator. If you like technology, you can try the Java version of the simple mortgage calculator.

Pensions

Nobody likes to think about old age, but we'd all like to retire as early as possible. To do so, you need to have invested enough to give yourself a decent standard of living once the wages disappear. Pensions are only one way of doing this, but you'll find plenty of advice on the Net.

MoneyWeb
(UK)

www.moneyweb.co.uk/products/pension

Overall rating - ****
Speed - Fast
Advertising Level - High
Free

If you can ignore the brash graphics, this is a useful site. A pensions audit uses Javascript to see if you are on-target for a relaxed retirement or if you need to be putting more aside.

It is not totally accurate and your own circumstances will have huge bearing but it will give you some idea of the ball park that you should be aiming for. State pensions are excluded from the audit, but the same site provides a real future value of state pensions projection.

Fidelity Investments
(US)

personal.fidelity.com/toolbox

Overall rating - ****
Speed - Fast
Advertising Level - Medium
Free

Another useful site from Fidelity who seem to have embraced the Web to it's utmost potential. Here you can use interactive calculators and worksheets to assist you with your pension planning needs.

Included are a retirement planning calculator, a contribution worksheet and a PlanMatch to compare popular retirement plans for self-employed individuals and small businesses. A raft of annuity calculators are designed to help you discover if you are going to meet your long term investment aims.

Tax

The mere mention of tax is enough to invoke
fear, dread and anger. But in thois age of
'customer' satisfaction, even the tax authorities are trying their best to make it as easy as
possible to take away our hard earned cash.
It's tempting to give each site a 'nil' rating
for its content...

Inland Revenue
(UK)

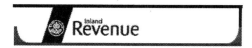

www.inlandrevenue.gov.uk

> Overall rating - ****
> Speed - Fast
> Advertising Level - None
> Pay for your entire working life

The official site of that group all Brits love to
hate - The Inland Revenue. Here you'll find
FAQs on all forms of tax queries, comprehensive information on all aspects of self-assess-

ment, the abilitiy to order, on-line - all those
helpful forms that are no longer sent out
automatically (it's your responsibility to get
the right forms), what's new at the IR and
technical help via access to documents on tax
law and reviews of taxation practices. Now
where's the page showing exact details of the
best loopholes?

Chartered Institute
of Taxation
(UK)

THE CHARTERED INSTITUTE
OF
TAXATION

www.tax.org.uk

Overall rating - **
Speed - Medium
Advertising Level - None
Free

This site is split into two main sections: tax for
the beginner and tax for the expert. The begin-

ner's section includes a tax-tip of the week, tax information and publications, how to pick a tax advisor, FAQs, an explanation of self-assessment and a list of tax enquiry centres. If you feel like lightening the load a little, and who wouldn't, take a look at the tax jokes and quotes, and if you wear an anorak, the history of tax in the UK.

US Tax Code Online (US)

www.fourmilab.ch/ustax/ustax.html

Overall rating - **
Speed - Fast
Advertising Level - None
Free

Want to know why you have to pay as much as you do? Here's a document that'll explain it all, if you are an expert in double-speak. It is the complete text of the United States Internal Revenue Code.

It is fully searchable, and hyperlinks have been inserted for the most useful jumps around the heavy reading. When printed, this document covers more than 6,000 pages, so searching online for that way of saving tax could be worthwhile and save you backache at the same time.

IRS
(US)

www.irs.ustreas.gov

Overall rating - *
Speed - Fast
Advertising Level - None
Pay throughout your life

A little shabby and definitely downmarket. The crux of the information is put across in the form of a daily newspaper called the, wait for it, "Digital Daily". According to the designers it is the "fastest, easiest tax publication on the planet". Well they would say that wouldn't they!

You can learn more about how federal, state and local taxes "work for you" (hah), join the IRS corporate partnership (hah) program and find out how to set up in business so they can improve their revenues. And, ever helpful, if you've 'discovered' that you owe more tax, you can fill in an on-line "e-file" and take advantage of direct debit payments. There doesn't however, seem to be similar help if you are due a refund!

TAX*interactive*

Learn More About How Federal, State, And Local Taxes Work For You.

Technical Analysis

Decision Point

www.decisionpoint.com

Overall rating - ****
Speed - Fast
Advertising Level - None
Pay with free sections

A top notch site for learning and improving your technical analysis skills. One of the largest collections of free tools to help you time the world's stock markets. The tools you have to pay for are, as the site says, "unique and affordable".

Prime stock market index charts, which are updated every day, are complimented by advice from newsletter publishers. Apart from helping you with your investment decisions, this presentation of advice with data will help you hone your own skills. When combined with the Technical Analysis Short Course, you'll find this site a good place to start.

Other features include daily market, stock and mutual fund summaries, historical charts and a weekly chart spotlite (focusing on one index, stock or industry), free mutual fund charts updated daily, relative strength ranking charts updated weekly (102 industry groups) and a useful glossary.

The main pay-to-receive feature is the Decision Point Alert which give daily commentary, analuysis, market stats, stock market timing advice and forecasts.

chartpatterns.com

www.chartpatterns.com

```
Overall rating - ****
Speed - Fast
Advertising Level - Medium
Free
```

If you are new to technical analysis or want a refresher on patterns then head over to this site. You'll find everything you need to know about the main patterns found in technical analysis. The more complex patterns are not covered, however.

chartpatterns.com

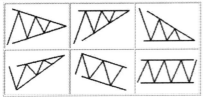
The analysis basics are given for symmetrical triangles, wedges, ascending and descending triangles, flags and pennants, rectangles, head and shoulders and the effects of volume. Sample charts, with discussion, are presented for each on a separate page.

Traders World

www.tradersworld.com

Overall rating - ***
Speed - Medium
Advertising Level - Medium
Pay with 30 day free trial

The online version of the printed magazine which appears quarterly on the newsstands.

As with the print version, the web site concerns itself with the trading of stocks, commodities and options with mathematical technical analysis. These tend to be more than simple pattern recognition, and techniques developed by Gann and Elliot frequently appear. There are also many articles covering new models and techniques.

Oddly, the online version offer weekly content changes, which is more frequent than the 'real' edition. The latest articles and interviews appear on the site with software, hardware and book reviews. Don't worry if you think you've missed anything as back issues are available on the site.

Technical Analysis of Stocks and Commodities

traders.com

Overall rating - **
Speed - Medium
Advertising Level - Medium - high
Pay with free trial

A neat URL for such a long title. This is another online version of the printed word, and there's little difference between the two. Indeed a large part of the site is given over to telling you what's in this month;'s issue of S&C - a table of contents, FAQs and a novice traders notebook. A plus is the ability to search the site, but this is limited to the subject categories given in a drop-down box.

International Federation of Technical Analysts

ww.ifta.org

Overall rating - **.
Speed - Medium
Advertising Level - None
Free

Marginally better offering than the STA. Again it is centred on itself, and you'll find plenty of information on the IFTA, but also a few resources.

The federation is dedicated to providing a centralised international exchange for information, data and business practices related to technical analysis - so the Internet should be an ideal medium.

You can read the latest IFTA newsletter and access previous issues, as well as join their E-mailing list. Two of the most valuable areas are the FTP site for downloading resources and links to the Technical Analysis Societies around the world.

Market Technicians Association

www.mta-usa.org/

```
Overall rating - *
Speed - Fast
Advertising Level - None
Free
```

Yet another site built for committees. Two of the stated main goals of the association are to educate the public about the use of technical indicators and to encourage the exchange of technical information.

Sadly the site goes little way to achieving these objectives. So much is possible in this area and the associations seem to have been left standing by the commercial sites such as Decision Point and chartpatterns.com.

Society of Technical Analysts

www.sta-uk.org

Overall rating - *
Speed - Medium
Advertising Level - None
Free

A front page for the society (as opposed to a home page). You can find details on the society itself but very little else other than links to other sites (not all directly related to technical analysis). About the STA, how to become an STA member, training to qualify for the STA, STA briefings, contact the STA committee, that sort of thing.

Ten Essentials
of On-line
Investing

Do...

1. Start to perform your own research. You have always intended to do it rather than take in other people's recommendations - but now, with the Internet as a tool, it is quick, easy and dirt cheap.

2. Cross reference all the information that you find.

3. Use an on-line broker and start cutting your cost of dealing. This means your investment will show a profit earlier and give a direct return for your time invested.

4. Take the time and effort to open an Internet bank account. The banks may not be up to full speed with the Internet just yet but it is the way of the future.

5. Take time to practice before you go "live". Investing on the Internet is basically a do-it-yourself programme and if things go wrong you've got no body else to blame other than yourself.

Don't...

1. Believe everything you read on the Internet. The cost of publishing something on the World Wide Web is minuscule and a good fraudster can publish an impressive Internet site one day and disappear forever the next.

2. Try and be the first to invest in the next big thing. There is a good chance that you will find this is a fraud. Why not accept that you may make slightly less money but be in the second wave of investors.

3. Pay for information that you need straight away. Look around the World Wide Web, it is absolutely huge. Somewhere out there what you are looking for is going to be available free of charge.

4. Give up at the first hurdle. Expect to come across a few difficulties before your system of investing on the Internet runs smoothly. You are dealing with a relatively new technology and advancements are being made every day. Stick with it and you will find yourself ahead of the field.

5. Invest in anything *just* because it has "Internet" or "On-line" in the company name. Silly money is being paid for Internet related stocks and it is going to end in tears. Make sure that they aren't yours.

Understand Shares in a Day
Second Edition

Shows how the share market really works. Inexperienced investors will learn: ❑ About different types of shares ... ❑ Why share prices fluctuate... ❑ How to read the financial pages ... ❑ How shares are bought and sold ... ❑ How risk can be spread with investment and unit trusts ... ❑ How to build a portfolio of shares ...❑ The risks and rewards associated with Penny Shares

Once this basic groundwork has been covered, the book explores more complex ideas which will appeal to both beginners and more experienced investors alike.

Ian Bruce   *128 pages*
ISBN:1-873668-73-2   *£6.95/$11.95*

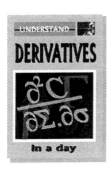

Understand Derivatives in a Day

Financial derivatives are used as highly-geared vehicles for making money, saving money or preventing its loss. They also have the ability to exploit volatility, guarantee results and avoid taxes. But only if they are used correctly.

Learn...How private investors get started... To Hedge, Straddle and control Risk... Ways to limit the downside but not the upside... About risk free derivative strategies... Trading Psychology - Fear, Hope and Greed... Also, the History of Derivatives; Currency Speculation; Long and Short puts; Tarantula Trading; and much more.

Stefan Bernstein
ISBN:1-873668-56-2

112 pages
£6.95/$9.95

Investing in Options: For the Private Investor

A book which shows you exactly how to 'gear' your money to provide more growth. Step-by-step it teaches how you appraise an options position, looking at the rewards and risks, and then how to execute a deal. There are plenty of examples to show you exactly how its done and how to trade profitably.

For the experienced options buyer there are examples of option combinations which can be used to create almost any desired outcome. With options you can make money whichever direction the market is moving.

Malcolm Craig
ISBN:1-873668-59-7

128 pages
£14.95/$24.95
Hardback

Create Your Own Website

Whether it is to showcase your business and its products, or a compilation of information about your favourite hobby or sport, creating your own Web site is very exciting indeed.

This book will help demystify the process of creating and publishing a Web site. Includes what free tools are available, how to create your own dazzling graphics, using a variety of free computer programs and who to talk to when it comes to finding a home for your Web site.

Mark Neely   *112 pages*
ISBN:1-873668-42-2   *£5.95/$9.95*

**Sex
on the
Internet**

**Golf
on the
Internet**

The **... *on the Internet*** series provides a detailed listing of the best sites in each category. Site addresses are given and all are reviewed in terms of content, layout and design, as well as the technical aspects such as speed of downloading, and ease of internal navigation.

Together, these handy pocket-sized references build into a complete directory of the World Wide Web

All titles £4.95/$9.95

Please complete the form below or use a plain paper and send to:

Europe/Asia
TTL, PO Box 200, Harrogate, North Yorks HG1 2YR, England
(or fax to 01423-526035, or email: sales@net-works.co.uk).

USA/Canada
Trafalgar Square, PO Box 257, Howe Hill Road, North Pomfret,
Vermont 05053 (or fax to 802-457-1913, call toll free 800-423-4525,
or email: tsquare@sover.net)

Postage and handling charge:
UK - £1 for first book, and 50p for each additional book
USA - $5 for first book, and $2 for each additional book (all shipments by UPS, please provide street address).
Elsewhere - £3 for first book, and £1.50 for each additional book
via surface post (for airmail please fax or email for a price quote)

Book	**Qty**	**Price**
	Postage	

☐ I enclose payment for _____ **Total:** _____

☐ Please debit my Visa/Amex/Mastercard No:

Expiry date: ☐☐☐☐   Signature:

Name: _____

Address: _____

_____

_____

Postcode/Zip: _____

invbk